To Howard
with best wishes
and
good traveling!
Ann Herlong

In the Wake of Saints and Sinners

A voyage where Saint Paul sailed, an odyssey where animosities whip across the seas unannounced.

Ann Herlong

ISBN Number 1-57087-215-5

Published By
First Watermark
PO Box 22854
Charleston, South Carolina

Production & Design By
Robin Ober &
Professional Press
Chapel Hill, NC 27515-4371

Map By
Ad Pro Graphics

Manufactured in the United States of America
99 98 97 96 10 9 8 7 6 5 4 3 2 1

For Gracie and Stephie,
and all my other grandchildren
in the hope that they will discover
how to sense the magic.

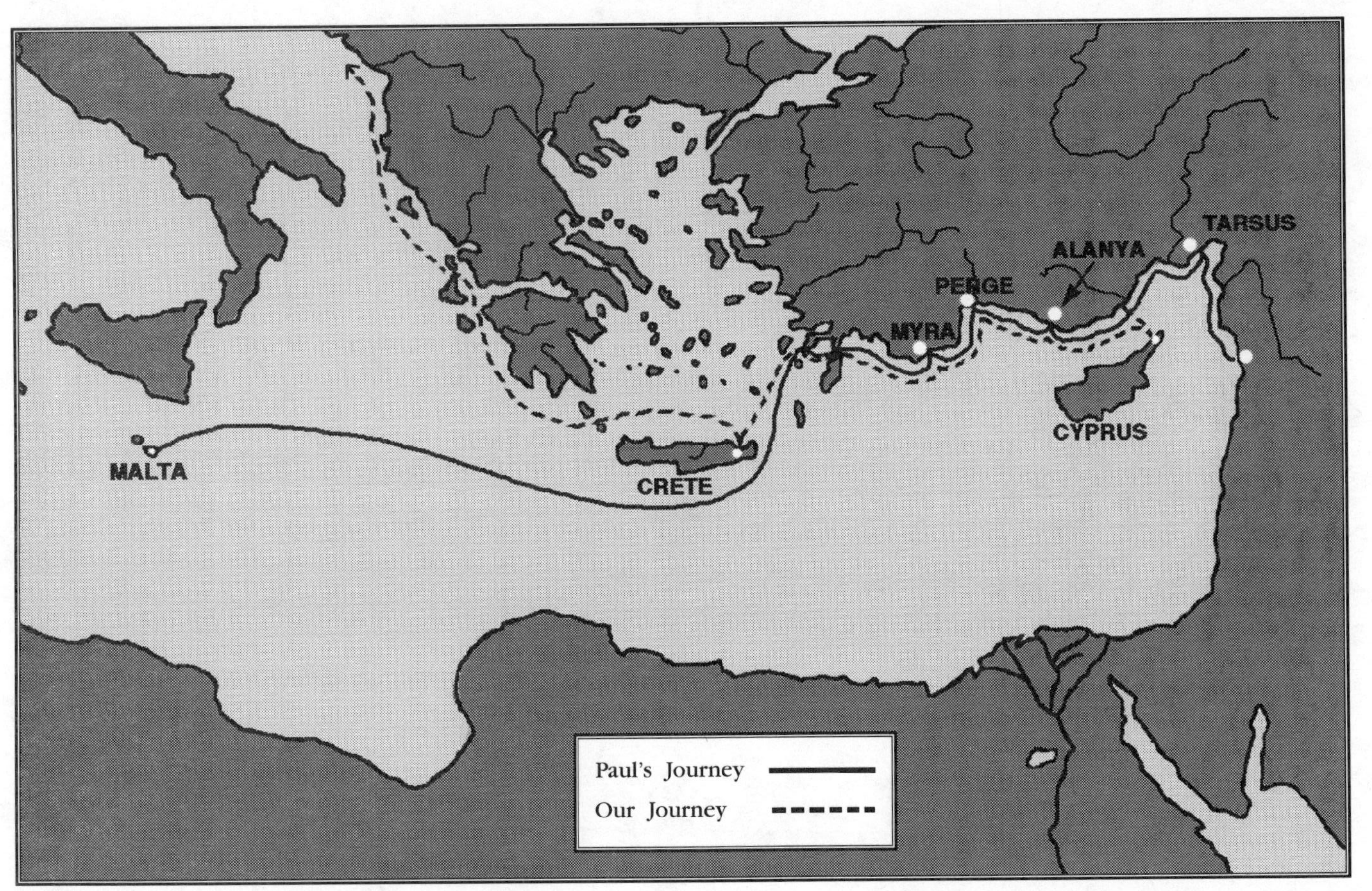
TARSUS
ALANYA
PERGE
MYRA
CYPRUS
CRETE
MALTA
Paul's Journey
Our Journey

Foreword

When RISE, a thirty-seven foot ketch, left Ashley Marina in Charleston, South Carolina, in May 1986, my heart went with her. She would cross the Atlantic and the English Channel. She would motor through the rivers and canals of France to reach the Mediterranean and then return to Charleston by way of the Canary Islands and the Caribbean. At least, that was the plan.

It was a dream of a lifetime for my son and daughter-in-law. They would be gone for one year, they said, and placed their careers on hold. They bid goodbye to families and handed over their financial affairs, telling me to pay their VISA bills as long as their savings held out. But when they entered the Mediterranean on the southern coast of France where they were supposed to turn west and head home, they hesitated. To the east were seas the ancients had sailed. Farther east was the cradle of Western civilization. Sensing the magic in those ancient waters, they changed their plans, yielded to the moment, and off they sailed – through the Greek islands for a year, around the Turkish coast for another year, and finally to Israel.

Three years later, I joined them on their way back from the Eastern Mediterranean. The course we took paralleled the final voyage of Saint Paul, his journey to Rome as a prisoner of Julius the Centurion, except for the shipwreck, I am happy to say. My story is one version of our voyage in the wake of the ancients. I am quite sure Steve and Susan have a story of their own, which is probably most unlike mine. After all, I was a mother-in-law sailing with adult children on a boat the size of a small motor home. Where would I sleep? What would happen to their privacy? How about my privacy? Sailing is twenty-four hour, around-the-clock togetherness. Could we live amicably in such tight quarters for six full weeks?

I began my story for all the students I have taught – ninth, tenth, seniors and college freshmen – who were forced to listen to me extoll the virtues of Odysseus, imagine the escapades of Dionysus, and describe civilizations that affect them to this day, even in their world of MTV, Hootie and the Blowfish, and Die Hard movies.

In addition, I needed to think through the history for myself and clarify the time-line of the civilizations which had developed and flowered around the Mediterranean. Except for the well-known Greek and Roman, I wanted to know which civilizations had made an indelible imprint on my own thinking. Whose customs had I seen practiced in remote harbor towns, I wondered. Were they Persian or Judaean? Were they Minoan or from some far-away Asiatic tribe? Whose rituals a thousand years old or more did we practice in some lukewarm, contemporary way?

But the customs overlapped when I remembered my sail in the wake of the ancients, and I felt with the poet, " . . . . faces seen once always change into and out of each other." Thus, I came to believe with Eudora Welty that "travel itself is part of some longer continuity." The divisions between people became less distinct. Their differences intertwined. The civilizations of the past and the present fused together

in my mind, and I decided in many ways we all live like that – sailors and landlubbers, young and old alike – we live in the wake of saints and sinners.

Faces seen once change always
Into and out of each other;
"You . . . are what I have witnessed.
You are all faces seen once."

– James Dickey
from POEMS 1957-1967

In the Wake of Saints and Sinners

1
The Voyage Begins

A hair-raising beep jars me out of my seat behind the wheel. The boat rocks and I lose my balance. My arms flail the air and my feet swing as if unattached to my body. I tumble headlong into the cockpit.

"Everything okay out there?" Steve asks, peering through the companionway door, thinking his mother on watch in the Mediterranean has fallen overboard.

"All's well," I say, but everything is not okay. I am numb with fatigue. I had arrived by plane on the island of Cyprus twenty-four hours earlier and before that hadn't slept in days. I was too excited about coming to this part of the world. When the plane touched down, and I saw soldiers standing along the tarmac, I was reminded that things are never okay in the Mideast. For the moment the winds have picked up and pushed our boat east. We are sailing toward the coast of Syria.

"Just off course a bit," I say and click the remote control, a device I hold tight in my hand, a plastic box somehow connected to the steering wheel. It's only plastic, but it's our umbilical cord to the West, a contraption that will hold us off the unfriendly shores of the Mideast and keep us on our way to the southern coast of Turkey. I click the box again and hold my breath. It works. The remote control engages, the electronic self-steering at the wheel responds, and within seconds the bow moves ever so slightly. I check the compass. We are heading again to Turkey.

"You want Sue to take over?" he asks, his voice tinged with what I construe to be sympathy but is probably closer to frustration. "I'll wake her." He offers to wake up my daughter-in-law who is scheduled to take the wheel in another hour. Since I'm here to prove something to the younger generation and certainly to myself, I assure my son I can handle my watch until she takes over.

This voyage from Cyprus to the coast of Turkey, a country friendly to the West, is only a distance of fifty nautical miles, but the trip seems longer, more like two hundred and fifty miles, as I imagine the Mideast to my right. Syria, Iran, and Iraq are looming dark and ominous over there, like a Rorschach ink blot in my brain, too close for comfort when you're sailing a thirty-seven foot sailboat with "Miami, U.S.A." painted on the boat's transom.

I check the chart Steve has spread out on the cockpit seat before me, hold tightly to the mainsail halyard, and pull in the jib as a matter of habit. In front of me the chart is a mere piece of paper, of course, but it represents the difference between the Mideast and the friendly West. On that piece of paper, buff represents land; white means free, open, international waters. Green warns me that sharp impenetrable rock can rise up without warning.

Steve has more faith in the chart than I do. When I look at our destination circled in red, which is nothing more than a tiny dot beyond the vast white and green on a piece of paper, I think of the monsters who dwell in the sea beneath us. One is a creature with six heads, each head armed with three rows of sharp teeth and each barking like a dog. Scylla, as I remember the myth, is the one that reaches for ships and seizes the crew. Swallows them up like tiny morsels. I hear the sea hissing around our boat and think of Chrybdis, a shapeless mass that swallows the waters three times a day and then belches, spews it – us – forth again.

We are sailing where ancient mariners accepted the danger and prayed to the gods for their safety since they had no red, green or buff to warn them. They had no charts. No paper. Charts were kept in their heads.

Following a chart on any sea is an act of faith, I decide as the wind settles down and I drift somewhere in the white glow of a stupor. Yes, following a chart is placing your trust in people you don't know, I resolve, people like aerial photographers, unknown chartmakers, graphic artists. If we were using our GPS (global positioning system), Steve's latest electronic, computerized navigational equipment – which we are not because we are sailing like the ancients, but if we were – we'd still be placing our trust in the unknown. We'd be placing our faith in modern technology such as expensive computer chips, incomprehensible computer programs and whirling satellites that pass over our heads, sending back full-color images from somewhere in outer space.

It's hard to imagine the Phoenicians sailing the middle sea using nothing but the stars. They read the swells by day and the stars by night as they sailed out into the Atlantic and down the coast of Africa to fill their ships with ivory, gold and wild exotic animals. How could they possibly place their faith in sea stories handed down from generation to generation?

Having no such faith, I stand, tall and straight, forcing myself to peer ahead through the darkness. The cabin top, wet with sea spray, glows under the mast light that shines down from fifty-two feet above. Beyond our bow, nothing is out there, only the jet black night, I hope. No other lights are visible. We're alone. No other ships sail with us; no other vessel crosses our path in the dark. In other words, we are safe; we are in no danger of colliding with another ship in the Eastern Mediterranean, I guess . . . .

I fight sleep, aware that many a luckless mariner saw the lights of another ship when it was too late; many an ancient forgot to keep watch and ended his life shipwrecked on the reefs, his bones lying with the bones of others who couldn't stay awake, didn't keep watch, and instead yielded to the gods. After all, it was the business of Somnus, the Greek god of sleep, to cast his spell and alter judgment.

When at last I sit behind the wheel again, I'm in a cold stream of sea water flowing from the forward deck. The blanket I wrapped around my legs when I came on watch is soaked. My jeans are heavy and soggy, but with resolve I sit, unflinching, determined to adjust to conditions that would be unthinkable on land. Sailing on the sea changes one's priorities, I muse philosophically. Comfort moves far down the list, I decide. Recognizing that sailing changes the attitude toward creature comforts, I suddenly remember what Beryl Markham said about the perspective she gained about her place in the universe while flying a tiny plane alone. The famous woman aviator, flying high above the sea and aware of the immensity of sky and sea, said she saw the "alchemy of perspective" reduce her world and all her other life to "grains in a cup."

I begin to understand what she means. My world is shrinking and I acknowledge a truth the ancients accepted all along: a ship on a big ocean is infinitesimal, a drop in the bucket, a trifle, a splinter. I look around at RISE and am reminded that any ship can be engulfed by the maelstrom at any moment. Whirlpools and eddies swirl, if not in the sea, certainly in the imagination. Satyrs and bacchanals throng around a boat. The sounds are intensified. Splashes and gurgles become hisses and snarls. Wordsworth was right: you can " . . . . hear old Triton blow his wreathed horn."

The wind shifts and the boat rolls to starboard. I click the remote and thankfully the automatic pilot engages, but this time the boat points too high. As a result, we lose the wind altogether and the big genoa hangs in midair, buffeting and luffing. The lines go limp; the heavy steel blocks collapse against the stainless steel plates. Raw metal clangs against raw metal, a sound that would wake up the dead, and soon Steve pokes his head through the cockpit door, looking at me strangely through one open eye. They are as exhausted as I am, having just sailed from Israel to Cyprus to pick me up for this leg of their voyage back to Italy.

I yank at the jib sheet and like a flash adjust the mainsail. Within seconds the disgruntled captain disappears to his bunk below, the genoa fills, and the boat sails smoothly under full sail. The sky is clear. I try to overcome my first night jitters by remembering what I had read about our destination: ". . . once the fertile ground on which the Seven Churches of Asia Minor were planted," I had read in the brochures. "A land where East met West, where Persian and Greek, where Jew and Roman walked the same streets, a land of omens and divinations, of gods and soothsayers."

My favorite story was about Alexander the Great who planned his campaign to India while he camped out along the coast of Asia Minor. More specifically, his generals planned the campaign. They mapped out the bloody strategy while he sat, wasting away in a harbor town called Phaselis. Later we would anchor in that harbor and learn there's a marble bust there, the one Alexander kept by his side. The story goes that on winter nights when he was melancholy and distracted, he put his arms around the statue of Aristotle, his teacher, and cried. We would find the harbor melancholy, silent, and overgrown and remember the sound of the tall pine trees humming in the breeze. And the fallen marble bust of Aristotle.

But the story that determined the course Steve would plot on the chart and our every stop for the next six weeks was the story of Paul the apostle who sailed this way on his way to Rome.

"That's what we can do," Susan had said the morning we left still holding her cup of tea.

"**What's** what we can do?" Steve had asked, his head buried in pilot books and charts at the navigation table.

"Follow Paul's final journey," she said.

"Paul who," I asked myself but I said nothing since my mind was still reeling from the shock of armed guards and border patrols thus hardly focused on early Christian martyrs.

Steve lifted his head and asked the same question: "Paul who?"

"Oh, you know," Susan explained. "Paul the apostle. He crossed Asia Minor on muleback and on foot. Then he sailed to Rome to carry Christianity to the West."

I suddenly recovered, "I thought he went to Rome as a prisoner."

"He did," Susan explained patiently, "and we can follow the same route."

The discussion had jogged my memory enough to offer another tidbit of information: "But his ship was caught in a storm if I remember correctly, and shipwrecked."

"Forget it," Steve told Susan and went back to his pilot books. But Susan's idea prevailed, and we would follow Paul course to the site of the most famous shipwreck in all of Christian literature.

In the darkness, I see nothing ahead of us; nevertheless, I suddenly have an uncanny feeling of uneasiness. If I didn't know better, I'd swear something is on the sea with us, but I can't call Steve. How could I tell him about a fear based on my intuition? I tell myself I have been through twenty-four hours of culture shock. I tell myself I feel jumpy and nervous because we're sailing too close to the Mideast. I am being foolish, but I am certain I sense a presence with us on the sea. Intuition?

It's true. When I look ahead, a cluster of lights hovers over the sea. One moment I see lights, but the next second they disappear. I check the chart for an island, land, some reason to see lights on the open sea, but there's nothing on the chart, only the wide band of white that represents international waters that are deep and safe. Fishermen on the sea at night? Hardly. There aren't enough fish left in the Eastern Med to bring a fleet out this far. The nearest channel for oil tankers and aircraft carriers is far to the south, along the coast of Africa between the Suez Canal and Gibraltar.

I fight the urge to scream for help.

"If you see lights . . . ," Steve warned when I took over the wheel at ten o'clock.

"I should call you," I suggested.

"No, no," he said as he went below, giving in to exhaustion. "You can handle it. All you have to do is determine its direction."

"How?"

"How what?"

"How do I determine its direction?" I asked. "How do I know which way another ship is going?"

I had taken lessons in piloting with the rest of the family, but on a lake in central South Carolina we never had to worry about freighters or oil tankers or submarines that emerge like gray humps out of the sea.

Steve repeated the litany we had learned together: "You determine the direction of a ship at night by the position of its masthead lights."

"Okay," I said, "Okay." I remembered the lessons on Lake Murray. "Look for the two masthead lights," I repeated. "Two white lights."

"If you see two lights, one in front, the other in back, one higher than the other, the ship is passing by, going the other way."

"But if the lights line up, we're in trouble."

"We could be," he said, shrugging his shoulders. "It's probably coming straight at us."

"If the two white masthead lights line up to form a central range, the ship is coming at us," I said.

Steve nodded. "That's right, Mom. And it's probably bigger than we are. It will be your job to get us out of the way."

The lights hang over the water in front of our boat. Dots double and quadruple before my eyes, but I wait, and then slowly, ever-so-slowly, I can distinguish two separate masthead lights which come to be half a football field apart, one higher than the other – two separate lights. Two distinct lights. One in front. One on the stern. It's clear that we will not collide. The ship is crossing our path far ahead and going in a different direction. I stay on course and sit tall behind the wheel, proud of myself.

But such decision making on the sea takes it toll, and feeling the pressure, I look into the darkness to clear my brain then breath the salt air deeply to calm my frayed nerves. Minutes pass. It may have been only seconds. I may have dozed off, but when I gain control of my senses again, I am staring directly into another cluster of lights.

This time the masthead lights are lining up; the lights are clearly and unmistakenly forming a central range. I watch, frozen with disbelief and paralyzed as two white lights become ONE light, which enlarges and enlarges as it moves steadily toward us. This ship is coming straight for us.

I refuse to believe and kneel into the wind on the high side of the cockpit. But when I close my eyes to test my hearing, I recognize the deep, ominous rumble of the diesel engines and there's no doubt in my mind: it's a vessel pushing through the swells straight for us. When I get brave enough to open my eyes, green and red hull lights blink at me.

"Steve." I click the remote control, knowing I'm in trouble. I click again, but our bow refuses to move. My suspicion is correct: the automatic pilot at the wheel refuses to respond.

"Ship, dead ahead," I scream as I grab the wheel to hand steer, but the cords on the auto pilot hold tight.

"Steve," I scream again. He gets the message, takes one leap up the companionway ladder, jumps across the cockpit and yanks at the web of cords holding us. Susan has heard the commotion. She leaps up and runs to the forward deck as if she can hold off disaster singlehandedly by waving her arms. Within seconds the blue searchlight blinds us all as it flashes over the seas. The large ship is warning us, but it's too late.

Steve fires our auxiliary engine, his eyes darting from instrument to instrument. His hands move like the hands of a surgeon as he maneuvers us away from the ship, now only yards from our bow.

"Let her go," he yells, telling me to let the sheets fly,

ordering me to release the sails that hold us on course. I manage to follow orders, and we move out of the ship's way with only moments to spare. The large vessel picks up speed as if to make up for lost time and chugs on toward the Mideast.

We sit in the cockpit speechless and immobile. "Could have been a Syrian warship," Steve supposes. In the panic, none of us has identified the ship's flag.

"Or an Israeli gunboat on patrol." I have read and prepared enough for the cruise in the Mediterranean to know about the tensions in that part of the world. The situation is as volatile as it had been for thousands of years. Animosities have not changed.

"Could be the black market delivering munitions to the Mideast," Susan says. "Could be guns and ammunition. Could be a ship bringing food."

"Or medical supplies," I say, but I don't believe the ship is on a humanitarian mission, not for a minute.

"He's probably as relieved as we are," Steve mumbles as he checks the compass direction. We nod our heads in agreement and sit huddled in the cockpit waiting for dawn, knowing about the animosity around us and feeling small and insignificant on that sea. Like the ancients, we hope whatever is out there will look kindly upon us. We realize that we, too, need the protection of the gods.

2
Bitter Lemons

I had felt the depth of mistrust in the Mideast while we were in Cyprus. On that island, I learned there was so much hatred and suspicion that the Greeks lived in the south while the Turks were confined to the north. Although NATO forces patrolled the border between the northern sector and the southern sector, peace was tenuous. On Cyprus animosity was a gaping, open, interminable wound.

When we told the young female clerk in the marina office that we were taking a one-day bus trip to the northern sector before we sailed away, she turned her cold, dark eyes upon us and said, "There is nothing to see in Turkish Cyprus."

"We'll be gone for only one day," Steve explained, demanding his passport which she had locked away. With boats from around the world sailing into its harbor, and Lebanon and Syria only one hundred nautical miles away, Greek Cypriots were cautious; they held passports as security.

"We're only going to visit old monasteries," I said, thinking the religious angle might appeal to the clerk's Greek Orthodox leaning.

"There is nothing to see." She was sullen and grim as she returned our passports. But later she appeared unannounced at our boat. You can imagine our surprise.

"Tomorrow," she said, "when you travel to the north, you make picture for me." She handed us drachmes. "Please?"

Susan explained that of course we would take pictures, but we could take no money from her. Nevertheless, Aretoula insisted on a business deal, forcing the drachmes into Susan's hand and showing us snapshots she had brought with her.

"I live in the northern sector until I was ten years old," she said, pointing to a farm house in the picture. There was green grass on the mountainside and a herd of white sheep encircling a cluster of carob trees in the valley.

"My father, he make grain. Next door was Turkish farmer. The children, we play together. I go once to a Turkish wedding. We sing, We dance together. Once they come to see our church, beautiful old church. But things change after the Turks invade."

We learned that families had lived in harmony for years on Cyprus until the Turkish army from the mainland invaded in 1974. Family was set against family, village against village and Aretoula's family fled to the south, the part of the island which became the Greek sector.

"After that we never trust the Turks," she said, her hatred reflecting centuries of invasions.

"This island is Greek, but I cannot cross the border and go north to my home," Aretoula said. Her voice was tense and bitter. "It is my home. It is where I was born, but I cannot go there."

Steve cleared his throat. Susan could only speak her name, ". . . Aretoula . . ."

"You go," she said, unfolding an old worn map she had marked for us. "I tell you where. I tell you how to outwit the Turkish border guards."

On the bus to the NATO check point, I sat by an old woman dressed in black, her gray hair drawn back in a bun at the nape of her neck. When I smiled at her, she looked away. She was no Aphrodite, that was sure.

Aphrodite, the ancient love goddess, was born of the seafoam on this island. Standing gloriously naked in her marble temple, she was worshipped for centuries on Cyprus. Her cult had spread to Asia Minor, then to the entire Greek civilization and thrives in our own America to this day. I smiled to think of magazines and movies back home where the sexual and erotic thrive in ways even the sensual Greeks could not have imagined.

When we arrived at the check point, Susan followed Aretoula's instructions and marched into the small building to face the Turkish guards and immigration officials. Whatever she said or did worked because she came out smiling. Our passports were stamped and in her hand were the keys to a car from SUN-O-CAR rentals.

"But we've got to be back by dark," she warned. "The checkpoint closes at dark."

We found the farmhouse and the quiet valley Aretoula had described. We ate a lunch of Turkish bread and Greek sausages while Susan took pictures. By early afternoon we were far to the north where we spotted Saint Hilarion's Castle perched between two peaks on the Kyrenian Mountains.

"It's a Christian saint who died there," I explained, holding in my hand a book about Cyprus.

"Maybe so," Steve said, trying to concentrate on the road, since he was having to drive British style, on the left hand side. "That may be so, but he's not there now."

We all looked to the top of the mountains rising at the northern coastline, sharp jagged peaks, and the monastery hiding in the clouds. "He's not there because the Moslems claimed he was one of theirs," he said. "They stole his body and buried him somewhere in the Syrian desert."

There were two places we wanted to see: Saint Hilarion's Castle and the Tree of Idleness, a legendary place at the turn of the century while Cyprus was safe and secure as a British colony. "Its shadow incapacitates one for serious work," a British writer said. We envisioned tables of mustached, raucous Greek men whiling away their time under the tree, drinking coffee or sipping white cognac, playing cards, their laughter echoing up the mountain.

When we got there, strange music was twanging from loudspeakers hanging in the tree. The tables were covered with white tablecloths and fresh flowers adorned the tables. The square around the tree was now a restaurant. Turkish men sat drinking tea, their olive complexion, their black mustaches and dark eyes reflecting nomadic blood from Arabia. They gestured slowly, thinking before reacting. There was no laughter, no cognac, no cards. The Tree of Idleness was once again part of the Islamic world of unquestioned rule and order, a world most unlike the Western Greek world of sensual pleasure. The island had see-sawed back and forth between East and West for thousands of years.

We were silent on the way back to the checkpoint, trying to sort out the mistrust and suspicion and remembering Aretoula's dark eyes flashing with bitterness and hatred when she said, "We never trust the Turks."

3
Modern Turkey

At the first sign of Turkey, sculptured rock stood like monuments in the water. Behind the rock, great humps of mountains materilized like a mirage. A mist was rising over everything, turning the coast mauve then spreading across the sky turning the world violet and rose. Homer's "rosy-fingered dawn" mesmerized us as we motored quietly into Tasuca, the nearest fishing village. With our red Turkish courtesy flag flying high on the backstay above our much larger Stars and Stripes, we tied up at the quay between two boats in the fishing fleet, small open boats loaded with baskets and fishing nets, and waited for the customs officials.

Steve spent the morning putting our documents in order. Five papers would be inspected by five different officials and stamped in five different offices in proper order, but he'd never know which order was proper because in Turkey each port of entry establishes its own procedure.

"Just to be different," other boaters warned before we left Cyprus.

He listed the official crew – three Americans: the boat's captain, his wife, and his mother, all from Charleston, South Carolina. The boat's documentation was in order, along with proof of the captain's American citizenship, a document that would be inspected and discussed at length in a language none of us could understand.

"Act as if you do," the cruising friends warned.

"Don't smile," they said.

While Steve updated the ship's inventory list, Susan, who was a nurse before she became the first mate on RISE, carefully and methodically itemized all the prescription drugs in her medicine bag. She, as well as the rest of the world, knew that Turkish officials become testy if they suspect a boat is trafficking in illegal drugs. Sailors who travel along those shores believe stories about dark Turkish dungeons and cruel prison guards. Lifelong savings can be lost fighting the Turkish court system. The American Embassy, five hundred miles away in Ankara, could hardly save three unknown Americans who got into trouble.

"Nobody's here," Steve said, returning to the boat at midmorning. His voice was flat, his shoulders sagged as he tossed the documents into the cockpit. Papers spread across the seat; passports fell to the floor. He climbed over the gunwale and slumped behind the wheel.

"Whataya mean, 'Nobody's here'?" Susan asked, sticking her head through the open companionway door, looking at him as if he were engaging her in some perverse joke.

"I mean, Sue, that the customs officials are not here." His words were deliberate, his enunciation distinct as he forced his shoulders higher. "There . . . are . . . no harbor police here, Sue. I can't find the doctor who can lift our quarantine . . . or the harbor master who can stamp our passports. All the offices are closed. In other words, my dear, there are no Turks around this place who can let us in the damned country."

"What about Tarsus?" Susan asked.

Steve repeated her question, so short and curt I glared at him, thinking I should remind him of his manners. "What about Tarsus?" he asked. After an overnight sail in the Med the mornings are tense, I would learn. We were exhausted but refused to rest. We needed sleep but were too excited to nap.

This was, we had decided after much discussion, not to be just any cruise. As Susan suggested, we would follow in the wake of Paul when he sailed to Rome to convert the infidels. Our course would take us along a coast where the Roman Empire had spread to the Eastern Provinces, along the shores of the Asia Minor of antiquity. It was the coast where the bold spirits of ancient Greece had founded great cities and opened the way for Alexander the Great.

We planned to begin our voyage officially in Tarsus where Paul was born. "Did you ask about a bus to Tarsus?" Susan asked. Since we were still under quarentine, we could save time and go by bus. "The guidebook says we can catch a local."

Steve's voice was forced. "If we get clearance, Sue," he said, "and if we can find one person who can speak English, one Turk who can translate the goddamned bus schedule, we will go to Tarsus this weekend. Yes, we will. We will go see Tarsus if that's really where you want to go."

Susan looked at me, rolled her eyes back and whispered, "He always gets like this. He gets nervous. Refuses to speak the little bit of language he knows."

Looking at the dusty, sandblown fishing village where we had landed, I was dubious about the famous description of the city another one hundred miles east where Paul was born, the city where Mark Antony met Cleopatra in 41BC. The port and the river had long ago silted up and the city was left inland, high and dry.

"The barge she sat in, like a burnish'd throne, burned on the water," Shakespeare wrote. He said the ship was gold, the sails purple. Perfume filled the air along the banks of the

Cydnus River; Tarsians stood waving palm fronds, "Aphrodite," they called to Cleopatra. "Aphrodite has come to meet Dionysus."

Once the towns along this coast were wealthy trading centers. Prosperous merchants left with Tyrian purple to trade around the middle sea. Artists from the coast gave the world the art of glass making and our alphabet. As part of ancient Syria, this coast had donated powerful emperors to the East and learned men to the West. Towns along this coast nurtured three of the world's great religions: Judaism, Christianity and Islam.

There was, however, little evidence of oriental luxury in the harbor where we sat. In fact, the town seemed reconciled to its poverty, content to be hemmed in between the East and the West and flanked by the great Taurus mountains. We saw no highway, no way out except by a chalky-white road that led up the limestone mountain, a road that wound around boulders and disappeared behind clumps of scrawny shrubs. Who are the people of Asia Minor today, I wondered. What kind of people would live here, and if they tried to leave, find themselves following a road to nowhere?

Turks appeared at noon wearing khaki uniforms trimmed in luxurious red braid and waving to Steve to "come along." He assumed that's what they meant and followed.

"You can tell this is Turkey," Susan whispered.

"Must be easier to enter Heaven," I said, watching the officials who were unduly stern, inordinately regimented for the simple job of registering a foreign boat for a six-week cruise along the coast.

"Too many people here for the government jobs available," she said.

"Too many uniforms, you mean."

"They like to re-live the glory days of the Ottoman Empire." At the sound of a loud snap, a thump, I realized she had released the dining table from its upright position where it had been folded and latched during the sailing trip. The wall behind the table sparkled with crystal and silver. Before they sailed from Charleston, Steve had hung a mirror and built shelves to carry a touch of luxury across the Atlantic. When the dining table was folded against the wall, their crystal was safe, even in the worst of sailing conditions. After they crossed the North Atlantic, they had enjoyed dinner by candlelight. Motoring through the rivers and canals in France, they had drunk wine from crystal wine glasses.

While she ran the Dustbuster, I took the carpets from the floor, the cabin sole, shook them outside, and draped them over the lifelines. In the houses above us, other women were shaking and hanging their carpets over the balcony rails, their bodies hidden under flowing cassocks, their voices low. They were gossiping perhaps about us, the three foreigners from halfway around the world down at the quay on a boat.

Steve reappeared at midafternoon with our passports stamped and our documents signed – all except our health certificates. Susan raised her head from the top-loading refrigerator where she had been sorting the cartons of milk and juices, half of which had spilled while the boat was tilted over during the sail. "But that means we're still under quarantine."

"That's right," Steve said, his voice edged with anger. "We can't leave until the good doctor comes back from across that mountain."

"When?"

"Tonight. Maybe tomorrow. The next day if we're lucky."

"You know what means?"

"No, Sue. What does that mean?"

"It means we'll miss seeing Tarsus."

That night we were in no mood to go up to the local taverna; instead, we heated cans of Campbell's chicken noodle soup and read about Tarsus. Susan leafed through the cruising guidebook. "Says here there's nothing left of the old Tarsus."

In its heyday the old city was a melting pot, where East and West lived together in harmony. Roman soldiers guarded the Cilician Gates and patrolled the Imperial Highway that led north to Ephesus and south to Antioch. Tarsus, like other cities in the Eastern Provinces, was self-governing. Rich merchants traded iron ore for silk and gold, spices and ivory. Its citizens enjoyed all the luxuries enjoyed by the Athenians or the Romans. Jewish boys at age fourteen studied at the Jewish Temple in Jerusalem; Greek boys studied in Athens or at the university in Alexandria.

But the city where the famous apostle was born had been overrun by armies from the East and theWest. As the power of the Roman Empire waned, the wealth in Tarsus declined and the city that Saul called "no mean city" was caught between shifting alliances and hostilities, run over by the advancing Seljuks then claimed by the Byzantines. According to the guidebook, Tarsus became a battleground for princes and Moslem emirs who finally arose out of Arabia to overrun the coast. Finally, the historic city was doomed to be trodden into dust, not by the Islamic forces but by Western forces, the Christian Crusaders marching to Jerusalem in the eleventh and twelfth centuries. An industrial Turkish city has grown up over the historic rubble.

The next morning while Steve hassled with the doctor,

the custom officials and the Turkish bureaucracy, Susan and I went to the market. Wearing long skirts over our shorts in this remote area of a Moslem country, we went into town, fully aware that we were the only unveiled women for hundreds of miles. We wandered among the vegetable stalls where the locals bartered and traded as their ancestors had been doing for thousands of years and where aromas of the East filled the air with olive oil, thyme, crushed garlic, and dried fish. Somewhere up on the hillside amplified chants echoed from the minarets as the muezzins called the people to prayer.

We picked out a dozen shiny green cucumbers, a kilo of cherry red tomatoes, three tiny ripe melons, and a large blackish-purple eggplant, a vegetable the Greeks call "aubergine," the color of the middle sea. The Turks call it "palican," a word that's less descriptive, but the vegetable tastes the same in any language.

"You won't like them," Susan whispered, pointing to a large wooden barrel filled with olives floating in an acrid smelling brine. The young Turkish girl standing by the barrel insisted that I try them and before I could resist, she grabbed my hand. She scooped up a handful of olives and placed them in the palm of my hand. Susan was right; Turkish olives are small and shrivelled, bitter and unpleasant. But before we left, I smelled Turkish bread. Ah. Turkish bread is sweet and yeasty, sold warm and fresh, right out of clay-domed ovens where it is baked.

As we left the market, an old man with a face as brown and wrinkled as one of his figs in the wooden tray beside him looked up from the ground where he squatted on his thighs. He handed me something that looked like a stalk of wilted celery. I hesitated, not quite sure what to do, how to react to these people in this strange culture.

"Take it, Mom." Susan spoke under her breath. "He wants to give you something."

"What is it?"

"I don't know but take it, whatever it is," she urged, poking me in the ribs while we both smiled a fake smile, showing our teeth, grinning unconvincingly, I was sure. "It's a gift, Mom. He wants you to take it."

Smiling at us and nodding, the old man took a pale green leaf from the celery-like stalk and put it between his brown teeth. "See," he seemed to say, chewing the feathery leaf as if to show me the plant was safe and nontoxic. I followed his gesture, forcing myself to chew a raw leaf, remembering the warning about eating unwashed vegetables. I chewed anyway. The leaf tasted familiar and I suddenly recognized the faint hint of licorice.

"Anise? Is it anise?"

"I don't know, Mom. What is it?"

"Fennel, Susan. It's fennel," I said, thanking the old man, who seemed pleased that I recognized the herb, a plant the ancient Greeks believed gave courage and strength.

I had read that it keeps away hunger, that it keeps the stomach from growling, but I prefer the Turkish belief – a gift of fennel is a form of flattery. I bowed clumsily to the old man, feeling contrite, hiding my Western ignorance. I would like these people with the customs of the past thousand years and more, a living history long gone from the prosperous West. Yes, I would like the Turks no matter what the Cypriots said.

4
No Mean City

After Mark Antony's famous rendezvous with Cleopatra, Tarsus thrived beyond the city fathers' imagination. A river pooled below the city in a deep, natural harbor that provided protection for merchant ships from around the Roman world. Ships lay at anchor with bright decorations, each flying the emblem and the name of the land of its origin. The ships carried away rich iron ore from deep inside the Taurus mountains, while giant trees, felled by the million, were rafted down the Cydnus and shipped around the known world.

The city became proud and cosmopolitan after the Egyptian queen sailed her royal barge up the river to seduce the Roman general. They loved the pomp and circumstance she brought with her. They called her the goddess risen from the waves. "Aphrodite has come to revel with Dionysus for the good of Asia," Tarsians proclaimed in 41 BC.

We went to Tarsus after all. Twenty centuries after Cleopatra, we traveled there on a steamy bus accompanied by the wail of modern Turkish music. We arrived expecting some evidence of Egyptian splendor but found only Cleopatra's Gate which looked like a brick wall. We didn't believe the sign that pointed to a house where they say Paul was born. The guidebook was right. Old Tarsus is no more. Army after army has long since trampled the city into dust. Like Ephesus and Myra and other great cities of the first century, the port has silted up and left the city landlocked miles up the river.

"Why couldn't Paul's father have been a ship captain?" Susan asked on our way back. "It says here he could have been a wealthy Jewish merchant who exchanged grain from the rich irrigated fields on the banks of the Cydnus for sweet-smelling cedar from Lebanon, pomegranates from Pamphylia, and papyrus from Egypt."

"No reason he couldn't have been." I agreed. After all, early Christian literature says he was born in Tarsus, but scholars have no facts concerning his early life. His journeys across Asia Minor, through Greece, then finally to Rome are recorded in the Christian Bible and tell us that as an adult he knew what lay beyond the harbor at Tarsus. On the other hand, there's little evidence to support any assumption about Paul's early life. Although die-hard biblical scholars say Paul's father was a tent maker, there is little evidence to support that assumption.

While Steve slept on the seat in front of us, Susan and I concocted our version of a young Paul growing up in Tarsus. The cool wind was blowing through the open windows of the bus and somebody else was in charge of the driving; in fact, Steve slept, the bus driver turned down the music, and except for one old man in the back, we were alone.

We decided that Paul's family, like other Tarsians who could afford to do so, probably moved to the mountains when the heat of summer turned the streets to dust and reduced the river to a trickle because north of the city, the air was cool. In those days a mysterious illness like malaria could wipe out the population of an entire city, but in the mountains a family would be safe from the dreaded summer illnesses.

"Like Charlestonians who went to Hendersonville for the summer," Susan suggested.

Families came back to attend the annual summer festival, we decided. Paul's family probably came down with their kinsmen. In Tarsus the festival was a celebration in honor of Augustus. By the time the Jewish tribes arrived, the city was bustling, filled with vacationers and tourists: craftsmen from the Greek islands, cooks and dancing girls from Egypt, Assyrian perfume mixers, magicians, Roman legionnaires and officials, scribes and tax-gatherers. The market was a din of hawking and bartering. There was laughter, the music of flutes, the ring of cymbals. The city was bedlam.

In the midst of it all, Paul's sister, (Susan insisted there should be a sister in our story) a year older than he and tall like his mother, ran off with her friends, giggling as teenage girls do while catching up on the latest gossip. Paul stayed by his mother's side. He was a loner even at an early age, Susan decided. His Jewish friends had scattered for the summer, I decided.

"Don't forget the gymnasium. All the Gentiles were at the gymnasium." Steve woke up enough to add to our version of Paul's early life. The old man in the back of the bus was asleep. There was no one else around to question our facts, which was a relief.

In our story Paul watched his mother make her way through the market, away from the unclean food to the stalls of the Jewish tradesmen. There was something special he wanted to remember about her. Perhaps it was the way she moved, the grace, the elegance of the flowing cassock that covered her slender body. Perhaps it was the way she appeared to others: supreme and unapproachable in her veil, an Eastern custom she practiced as all Tarsian women did in those days. At home she was open and warm, as funloving and carefree as any Greek mother, but when she went veiled into the street, it was as though her veil conveyed upon her a mysterious authority, a power beyond his comprehension. (My courses in religion at Columbia College, a Methodist girls school, were finally coming in handy). As men and children, even the Roman soldiers, gave way for his mother, his heart filled with pride to watch her.

When he thought of leaving home for Jerusalem, Paul's anticipation was tinged with regret, but he would travel in the company of friends. Most boys in the large Jewish population in Tarsus went to school in the Hebrew capital. He would renew his friendship with Barnabas, a friend he made when he sailed to Cyprus with his father one summer. He had much in common with Barnabas. He, too, was a scholar who had learned the Jewish Law by heart. He, too, had sat at the feet of traveling philosophers like Ploutiades and Diogenes and heard poets like Artemedorus and Diodorus read from their work. Tarsus was a city that ranked with Alexandria and Rome as the city of scholars and thinkers; the academy was famous for arithmetic, rhetoric and astronomy.

"Come, Saul." The mother probably used his family name, his Jewish name to call a young Paul who was watching a carpet maker work his loom, intrigued by the weaver's flight of hand.

"Look, Mother. Look at the intricate pattern," he may have said, pointing to the detail being woven into the fabric.

"Son, come." His mother tugged at his arm, as any mother would, moving him away from the traveling preachers in their tattered and bedraggled cloaks who continually berated the worldly pleasures of Tarsian life, the earthly riches that Paul's family enjoyed. "Repent," they were shouting, their long dirty hair and unkempt beards emphasizing their contempt for material gain.

"Come along. Come away," his mother urged. "Help us. Come. Take these goods to the servants. Helene can have supper ready for us. We will stay in the city tonight and return to the hills tomorrow."

"Do you think father will surprise us and return today?" The young boy had sailed enough to know that the winds were out of the south; they were favorable, in fact, perfect for the return of his father's heavily loaded ships. He knew that a stiff following breeze could kick up any time from the southwest, a *sirroco*, the desert wind from Egypt that could bring the large ships up the river by nightfall.

"I think he will not return today, son. But we should not be disappointed. We must pray for his safety," his mother said, no doubt looking down at the harbor and out to the lumpy sea.

Climbing the steep steps to the family home, he passed white-washed stone houses that seemed to him to have been built into the hillside. He passed the synagogue which was strangely quiet. The day we imagined everyone was at the quay preparing for the festival: building platforms for the parade, decorating the streets with laurel, myrtle and evergreen, sewing costumes for the actors, preparing food: sheep flesh, goat flesh, young boar's head, calves' kidneys, pheasant and dove.

In his old neighborhood, his mother's friends, no longer veiled, chatted over the courtyard walls. Children played in the streets and old women dressed in black – always in mourning after the death of a husband – sat on the steps in the doorways. Paul could feel the coolness escape from the houses behind them as he passed the open doors.

"Paulus, is that you?" asked an old wrinkled woman sitting in a typical doorway on the shores of the Mediterranean. "Come, my boy," she said and motioned to him with one crooked finger. "Come. Jason will be so glad to see you," she whispered, careful that others did not hear. She tapped the top of Paul's head, making his red curls bounce. Jason's grandmother knew he was Jason's friend; she had overheard their discussions, their heated debates. She had learned to accept their friendship as normal in a city of diverse cultures where East met West.

We decided that Jason's family would be Greek, descendents of the original Ionian immigrants to the coast, the first Greeks to inhabit Asia Minor after the Trojan War. They were long-time residents; in other words, the blue blood of Tarsus. Jason's family told stories of a brave ancestor called Perseus, a god who wore the helmet of Mercury, which made him invisible. They sang songs about Perseus who sped over the sea "on winged sandals, flying swift as thought."

Paul's family was hard-core Jewish. His father's family had settled in Tarsus after fleeing Palestine two centuries before. They were Pharisees who had come with a tribe of kinsmen and received full Greek citizenship from a local king who was promoting the growth of his Greek cities in order to rival Ptolomy of Alexandria. He allowed the tribe to stay together in a close-knit group. It was fine with him if they remained fervent Jews. In fact, the tribe became members of the ruling class in a city that governed according to its own law. Paul's grandfather had been mayor, a burger, a city father, and had so distinguished himself in early Roman times that Caesar had extended full Roman citizenship to Paul's entire family.

When Paul's friend, Jason, returned from the gymnasium, his strong naked body glistening with oils, Paul no doubt greeted him solemnly. In our story they walked up another flight of steps to the pinnacle of the Acropolis that gleamed in the late afternoon sun. They talked of friends who would be leaving for university studies, pretending as young men do, to look forward to getting away from home. Paul would study at the feet of the great teacher Rabban Gamaliel; Jason would leave for Ephesus where he would study with Strabo, the renown Greek geographer.

By the time he reached the Temple of Apollo, Paul's legs were quivering. From all we know about Paul, he would have been shorter than Jason, more frail, weak for days after the strange malady seized him, came upon him without any warning. Even if he had worked out in the gymnasium as the Gentiles did, he would never have been a physical specimen like the young Greek whose shoulders were broad, whose muscles were well-toned. Paul must have looked at Jason and marveled. In his imagination he could hear the cries from the crowds that assembled at the games and looked at the athletes with their rolling chests, their indrawn stomachs, the hardened buttocks. The stadium rang with"Adonis! Adonis! Adonis!" Like all Tarsians, he knew the story of Adonis, the young Greek, so handsome, so athletic, so manly, so magnetic, that Aphrodite herself fell in love with him.

"Sixteen," Jason said, sitting beside Paul after performing the obligatory rites to Apollo, the pagan ritual they all performed without thinking, without any real feeling, unless they were sick or asking for a special favor.

"Sixteen?"

"Yes, sixteen. Sixteen years of age. We'll meet in Rome when we're sixteen, Paul. Just you and I. We'll sit in the agora by the Pantheon and continue our debates," Jason said.

"Perhaps," Paul said. He hesitated. "I doubt if I can leave Jerusalem. I'll be a Scribe by then, but I'll need another degree if I plan to come back to the synagogue as a teacher."

"You'll come back to Tarsus and do more than teach, Paul. You will lead the whole city. Like your grandfather."

"I'm not a messiah, Jason."

"You'll be the first Jewish governor of the Province, mark my words. Change is coming."

"The order of the world will change in our life time. You are right. But I am not a messiah."

"You're a born leader," Jason told Paul. "Everyone says that. You know it, too. You are a born leader."

But Paul had already jumped from the steps and run with his weakened legs to the ledge overlooking the harbor. He stood pointing to the river beyond.

"Look. It's father," he shouted. Tiny white dots appeared at the horizon. Sails. His father's ships were returning, laden with corn just in time for the summer celebration, just in time to feed the crowds who had come to the festival. The fields in the plains on either side of the river Cydnus were normally green this time of year, but the rains had come early this particular spring and after the corn was planted the earth had turned brown. In spite of all the pagan rituals, the gods had refused to send rain and the plants had withered in the summer heat. The stalks were still only knee high. To ease the shortage the city council had requested help from the Roman Governor. Augustus himself had answered with a gift of corn from Egypt, and Paul's father had been dispatched with two ships to carry ore in exchange for the precious corn from Egypt.

By the time Paul ran down the steps and made his way through the busy streets, his father's ships had lowered their anchors, according to our story. He stood back from the harbor while trumpets sounded and a tall Roman officer led a battalion of centurions along the quay. His father, clean-shaven and dressed in fine linens, bowed before the officials and handed the shipping documents, stamped and sealed, to the Emperor's emissary.

The arrival of his father's ships was impressive, a scene any teenager would remember long after he left Tarsus. With the day's protocol out of the way, the emissary turned to the young boy. "I've wanted to meet you, Paulus. I've heard so much about you from your father."

Paul was careful to speak Latin. We know he learned many languages and could use the appropriate one, whether it was Latin, Greek or Aramaic. His father obviously wanted the best education possible for his Jewish son. At thirteen Paul had probably already read the Hellenic classics.

"Come, Saul," his father said after the officer left, the centurions marched away, and the trumpets echoed in the distance. "Let's surprise your mother. Where are they? Go find your sister. We'll watch the pageant together as a family."

Paul had never been allowed to see the pageant, the procession of gods the Gentiles paraded before the crowds. His father, strict and unbending, had never allowed his family to watch the heathens boast about their gods and display their religious superstitions.

"You are old enough today," his father said. "Old enough to place the history of Tarsus in your heart. Place it in your heart forever. It is no mean city, Saul. It is your home, son. You must remember Tarsus. You must know always, no matter where you travel, you are Saul of Tarsus."

Long after midnight we stumbled aboard our boat, and for days poured over books we had brought with us. It's true that Paul's hometown was "no mean city." Roman historians and documented coins verify that Tarsus was anything but a second rate city in that part of the world. Julius Caesar entered the gates of Tarsus on his march from Egypt in 47 BC. After the assassination of Julius Caesar, Mark Antony took over the Eastern Provinces and bestowed the highest Roman privileges upon all citizens of Tarsus for their loyalty, their adoration of his Egyptian mistress, his "Venus risen from the sea."

Later Emperor Augustus showed a special affinity for the city by building a vast amphitheater specifically for the summer festival and presenting it in honor of the most famous Tarsian of the time, the philosopher Athenodorus who had taught the young Augustus. Athenodorus had been called to Rome as adviser and was thus adored by the Tarsians. He would have been honored at any festival. His words would have been printed on placards and waved to the crowd: "Know that you are free from all passions only when you have reached the point that you ask God for nothing except what you can ask openly."

Of all the Romans honored in the parade, Tarsians would have chosen Pompey, the Roman who had become larger than life, the general who was admired and revered because of his military conquests along the Cilician coast. Pompey would have been represented as a great general, brandishing his sword as he put down the pirates that held the coast captive, a danger so great before he came along in 67 BC that even Roman ships were afraid to pass that way. Trade with Tarsus was impossible until Pompey cleared out the pirates.

Before then the coastal outlaws feared no one. They even captured Julius Caesar and demanded a ransom. For that error in judgement they got no money but were captured and crucified instead. Pompey opened the seas and made travel safe again; Pompey marched to overcome the barbaric armies of Tigranes, a king of Armenia, and made Cilicia an Eastern Roman Province. It was Pompey who named Tarsus the regional capital.

The large Jewish population would have secretly and privately honored the Greek king who had made Tarsus a free Hellenistic city and invited the small band of Jews to settle there two centuries earlier. The king offered them full Greek citizenship and gave them the freedom to practice their Judaism. They would have watched the pagan parade knowing full well that they, the Jews, were Tarsian long before the Romans came along.

There would have been gods a plenty to honor at the summer festival; all the Caesars were gods. There were Asian gods to honor. Cybele, the Great Mother Goddess wrapped in snakes, would have been borne along in a platform drawn by tamed lions, as she had been since the days of the Phrygians, a thousand years before. Her cult had spread across the Aegean to Delphi where her mysterious black rock drew worshipers and mystics, madmen and oracles to blood sacrifices and wild, orgiastic dances. Her son would have stood on the platform beside her: Sabozius, who died and rose from the dead each spring with the rebirth of crops and vegetation.

Another goddess would have won any popularity contest sponsored by the festival; in fact, she was taking the pagan world by storm, a figure more benevolent than Cybele. She was the goddess called Isis, Queen of Heaven, who promised immortality, a better life after death, a promise that appealed to the slaves, the poor, the downtrodden. In the pageant her statue would have stood, madonna-like, on a simple platform, her head bowed ever-so-slightly, her bare breasts representing fertility, her gentle, reverent priest-like son standing with her.

To please the Roman soldiers, a minor god named Mithras would have been honored. Word was spreading about elaborate, complicated initiation ceremonies among members of the male-dominated cult. In the provinces they were saying that centurions participated in secret rituals. They were being baptized with holy water, it was said, and ate sacred meals of bread and wine. Mithras' arms would have been drenched in blood, for he was the slayer of the sacred bull from whose blood all life emanated.

Old Greek gods would have had their place, especially Perseus who appeared on Tarsian coins struck as far back as the sixth century BC, also Heracles, broad-built and muscular, who had performed his labors all over Asia Minor. Diana would have appeared in the figure of a woman, her robes outspread like wings, her feet barely touching the platform, a bevy of nymphs, graces, and fauns – all dancing about her in a circle. Wise Athena would have been on a platform, her golden veils drawn around her; naked Aphrodite would have been surrounded by tiny cupids. Zeus would have been sitting on a throne, grasping the thunderbolt in his right hand. Apollo, god of the sun, would have been ablaze in scarlet, Hades surrounded by demons.

Festival organizers had little choice about the climax of the festival. The finale was fixed, set in stone, repeated year after year. At the end of the day, one god and one god only was rolled into the amphitheater on a special platform. Ancient coins show the god standing on a lion with a divine eagle perched above him. Coins struck in the first century AD show the god with a combination of Eastern and Western traditions: draped in a Western Greek tunic and standing on a structure reminiscent of a pyramid in the East.

The platform would have been drawn outside the city gates and taken to a funeral pyre where a replica of the god was burned with glorious pageantry. Following the rituals, the chorus, the sound of the cymbals and the fiery conflagration, there would have been fireworks from the East, something to rival our thirteen-gun salute, a magnificent occasion befitting the god of Tarsus, the ancient Asian god who transcended into the heavens each year to be reborn and worshiped, to be glorified, to be idolized, to be adored by all Tarsians, to be worshiped as the god of Tarsus: Baal-Tarz, Lord of Tarsus.

5
In the Middle of a Corn Field

Sailing away from the fishing village after the doctor released us from our quarantine, we began our journey to the West. We crossed large bodies of water smooth as half-congealed Jello, often threading our way between massive rocks. At times we passed under the shadow of whitewashed houses clinging precariously to the side of the mountains.

We were "moving by momentum or force of gravity" or "coasting" as any dictionary would say. We were skirting the coast, sailing from port to port, exploring, "scouring," as if we were bicycling down-hill without using pedals or sliding down a snowpacked slope on a sled.

Proceeding "without great effort" is not something I ordinarily do, whether it's teaching composition to college freshmen, playing golf, or cooking for twelve, (or two for that matter) but along the coast of Turkey, with its clear, unruffled, turquoise water, I had no trouble letting go, moving with the momentum of the swells. Freed from the hassle of passports and the inordinate demands of Turkish officials, we happily succumb to their dimension of time, an Eastern dimension which, I would learn, is infinite and hypnotic. In the mornings we moved along the coastline in silence, reading, absorbing the scenery, contemplating. At midday we harnessed the power of our Perkins engine, much to the chagrin of our captain who much prefers to sail as the ancients did. In the late afternoons when the westerlies died off, we caught the offshore breezes and barely moved, hearing only the sound of water swishing against the hull and watching the feathery wake behind the boat.

By nightfall we were looking for a lagoon, a place safe from the unpredictable winds of the middle sea, as the ancients called that sea. We needed a protected anchorage where we could spend the night. We could hardly anchor the way Odysseus anchored his black ship, the same way all ancients anchored when the sun went down. They beached their boats. RISE's six-foot draft kept us off the shore itself but allowed us to enter remote, hidden places with only ten feet of water. When Odysseus entered an anchorage, he dug the nose of his boat right onto the beach and his men pulled the vessel out of the water. His cattle, sheep, and goats grazed on the mountainside while he and his men slept under the giant mainsail they had taken off the boat raised over them like a tent.

But we were rarely alone. Fishermen in small boats joined us; they'd beach their wooden boats painted blue in years past, the sides now streaked brown from rust. They would roll their slacks above their knees and work silently with great length of nets, never in a hurry, as if mending nets was a release from their problems, a way to forget their meager existence, to overlook the poverty around them. They spread their nets out on the rocky shore, never talking to each other and ignoring us.

They were men who tilled the earth on the rocky sun-baked mountainside. The land there produced nothing of value and in the summer they came down to the sea to fish, but there are few fish in the waters along the southern coast of Turkey and haven't been for centuries.

They came down the mountain for other reasons, we decided, the same reasons we had for an unhurried cruise along the coast. They came to connect with the sights and sounds of the sea, to think, to reflect, to connect with their inner thoughts.

While we sat anchored among their boats, Susan sometimes poured the Cypriot wine we had brought illegally into a Moslem country and kept hidden from the customs officials. We'd sit under the still and silent sky feeling guilty, like members of the cult of Dionysus since we had stashed away enough of the fragrant grape in Cyprus at fifty cents a bottle to last until we got back to Greece.

In one of those anchorages we thought we saw black and white dots weaving through the shadows on the mountain-side beside us, but soon realized the dots were goats picking their way over the rocks. The bells around the wayward kids echoed across the water, and the voice of the goatherd called to the strays. Such sounds as those haven't changed over the centuries.

Standing guard over us always was a pirate fortress. All along the way there would be small fortresses and large fortresses; ruined castles and towers, fortifications built on mountain tops by the sea. Some would be well-preserved, others reduced to rubbish by hordes of invaders from the East and the West. Most were not important enough to be listed in a travel guidebook, just lion-colored rocks glistening in the morning sun, always less picturesque than we had imagined; nevertheless, time after time we climbed up, trampled along the ramparts, and crawled into the circular towers where sparrows chirped unhappily since we had invaded their space. We'd hear the wind, always rising from the sea and whistling through the rock. We'd watch lone swallows riding the air current and hold our breath when lizards puffed their throats as if to warn us of danger coming from the sea.

For centuries pirates owned these waters. The barrenness of the hills forced people down to the coast but the sea brought no wealth. Since there were no fish, the people turned to piracy. Any ship passing by was expected to pay a toll. If a captain hesitated, he paid with an arm or a leg. If he refused, he paid with his head. Even if he gave in and paid the fee, he was left with nothing to take with him aboard his ship.

The outlaws could muster enough ships to sack any merchant fleet dumb enough to try sneaking by. In 67 BC it took three months of battle, but Pompey destroyed thirteen hundred pirate ships and captured four hundred others. When it was over, the Roman general had slain ten thousand marauders. Another twenty thousand surrendered to save their heads from rolling. After the slaughter, trade resumed with the Roman world and prosperity returned to a coastline that once flourished as part of ancient Syria.

Under Roman rule the fortresses were transformed and used as garrisons for soldiers. Roman architects added fine arches and built temples to the glory of Caesar. Outside the garrisons they added colossal amphitheaters and huge municipal baths. They carved elaborate triumphal arches to honor their generals. They lined wide streets with marble busts atop marble columns to honor the rich and powerful. The coast became a land of plenty, a Roman paradise.

When Mark Antony commanded the forces in the Eastern Provinces, he presented the coast to Cleopatra as a gift. Whether her wanton beauty coaxed it out of him we'll never know, but historians say there was a purpose in his generosity: he needed war galleys to put into battle against Caesar. War galleys required timber, and lots of it, so the valuable timber along the coast was felled and sent to Egyptian shipbuilders to build the war machines Antony would put into battle at Actium.

After Rome weakened and pulled out, others came to claim the fortresses and add their touch. The Byzantine civilization, that vast religious conglomeration that held Christianity together for centuries, thought the fortifications looked like a fitting spot for churches. Therefore, they rebuilt the Roman temples and added golden domes. On the ceiling they painted colorful frescoes; inside they placed icons of the Blessed Virgin Mary. They added mosaics, tiny pieces of glass that sparkled like precious gems. The mosaics have long since been shattered by vandals, but faded fragments capture enough of the late afternoon sun to remind us of the glory days of Byzantium.

After that, the Saracens of Arabia, riding swift steeds, stormed out of the desert. They crossed the coastal plains with cries of war echoing up the mountains. They scaled the fortress walls, threw out the Christians along with their icons, and declared the territory to be Moslem. They added cusped arches with inlaid stones of black and white and built minarets, slender towers from which the muezzin called the followers to prayer. Then they planted banana plants and orange trees around fountains that flowed quietly. In the chalky dust they created gardens.

Then along came the Crusaders, Christians on their way to save Jerusalem from the "infidels" in the eleventh and twelfth centuries. They came down through the center of Byzantium, reeking more havoc to Constantinople and Byzantine art, historians say, than the barbarians had inflicted upon Rome centuries before. The Second Crusade spent its time pillaging and plundering at random without the leader, Louis VII of France. The rag tag army didn't know it, but the king had abandoned them and slipped aboard a ship to sail to the Holy Land in more dignified company.

Leading the Third Crusade, Emperor Fredrick I Barbarossa fell into a gorge up in the mountains, they say, and drowned. The locals say his army as well as the corpse quickly disintegrated in the heat of the summer. No other Western army set foot on the coast until the twentieth century. The Ottoman Empire saw to that.

The coast was forced to adapt. The people surrendered to the foreign invaders to survive. They gave in to the pirates or negotiated. They created intricate alliances with the powerful. They sold their honor and bartered their allegiance in return for their lives. It's the price the helpless and the disenfranchised pay for survival.

Alanya is the most famous of all pirate fortifications on the coast. It was the control center for the entire lawless operation, its turrets so high a lookout could spot merchant ships far out to sea. This is a fortress you can read about in the guide books.

Within an hour we were climbing up what looked like a sheer rock face since Steve refused to pay a Turkish taxi driver his asking price. Up we walked, climbing, stepping over thistle, dodging turmeric.

"Keep up, Mom," Susan called from ahead. "It's getting late." Shadows were falling across RISE, far below in the harbor.

"We'll never get to the top before sunset." I admit my attitude needed adjusting.

"Yes, we will," Susan said. "We need the exercise."

"Hiking is not my favorite exercise," I said, huffing and puffing, when from behind the next rock, someone arrived to show us a quick way to the top (we assumed that was her message). We should have known she was no tour guide, no innocent goatherd, but we were unschooled in the customs of Asian beggars, unprepared for a woman "possessed of a demon." She waved us forward, so up we climbed, following her goats until she pointed to a wall, babbling in some unintelligible tongue, wild disjointed words that couldn't have been Turkish, I decided immediately. Perhaps no language at all. Her teeth were dark with stain and decay, her red hair matted around the yellowing skin on her face. How was I to know that old Moslem customs still exist, that a woman can be turned out of her home, abandoned by her family, disowned by a husband or her dead husband's family and left to beg on the streets for food?

"Steve. Susan," I called. They were moving ahead, unaware that they were leaving me in trouble with the beggar who grabbed my skirt.

"Steve," I screamed. "Money. Where is our money?" US currency had worked miracles in taxicabs and in the bazaar. Surely it could keep a beggar away until I climbed over the wall. "Give her money," I demanded, but Steve pulled out empty pockets in his jeans. He had brought nothing with him from the boat: no currency, no coins, nothing to give the woman, who looked more and more like an escapee from a mental hospital.

"Not even a dollar?" I smelled the stench of goat and rancid oils as she got closer. Urine filled my nostrils. She spat in my face.

"Run," Steve shouted and pushed me away from her. "Get over the wall." I knew he was yelling at me. I knew he meant for me to get over the wall and run, but I couldn't move, so he pushed me out of her range, all the while taking off his watch and offering it to her.

Knees shaking and heart pounding wildly, I did get over the wall – how, I'll never know – and within seconds I was lost in a crowd of German tourists. Among them I caught my breath and tried to stop shaking, but I felt guilty about leaving the woman on the hill. For days I glanced over my shoulder to see if she were behind me, but I had lost her.

"That's okay, Mom," Susan said the next morning, trying to make me feel better. "You were in good company. Paul had to fend off a beggar when he traveled here."

She was a slave girl who babbled when fits came on her, Susan had read. Her owners had put her on a leash and sold her services as a soothsayer to the rich. Whenever the slave girl heard Paul, she dragged at her leash as she tried to get to him. A lunatic frenzy would come over her. Of course, rumor had it that the traveling preacher, too, was a lunatic.

One day Paul stopped, fixed his eyes upon her and commanded the demons to leave her. According to the biblical story in the New Testament called Acts of the Apostles, the beggar fell to the ground, writing, wailing, snarling and howling – "spitting out the demon."

Our next stop was in the ancient city of Perge, a city of commerce and trade, very much a Roman bastion two thousand years ago, teeming with soldiers who enjoyed the extra pay, the per diem, for service at a post so far flung and remote. Roman emissaries enjoyed the quality of life there because the area had all the amenities of Rome: luxurious baths, exhibition matches between slaves and exotic animals as well as exciting chariot races in the largest stadium on the coast.

We wanted to explore the excavated city since we had learned from the Book of Acts that Paul had preached there. He, along with two other itinerant rabbis, Barnabas and John

Mark, chose to begin converting the Gentiles in Perge. In those days three traveling preachers coming into a port city was not unusual. It was not uncommon for the Cynics to rant and rave across the great cities of Syria, for priests and priestesses to clash their cymbals and wail their flutes in the streets. Fortune tellers, soothsayers, and magicians drove a thriving trade among the soldiers. Judaism was just one more religion the Roman governors tolerated, but Judaism was filled with fanatics who had recently started riots in Jerusalem. In fact, they had stoned one of their own and crucified another. The Jews were known as trouble-makers, but Perge was far away from the dissention in Jerusalem; the streets were calm and safe since they were policed and patrolled by a garrison of Roman soldiers.

When Paul's little band of rabbis entered Perge, they were traveling light with only their mantles, a change of linen, and a four-cornered ritual fringe shirt. They would have joined the small population of Jews gathered for the ritual washing of hands before prayer and the reading of the Law and the Prophets. We can imagine Barnabas, who by all accounts was a tall and stately Cypriot, his black beard falling half way down the front of his mantle. Paul, we know, was frail and restless; and John Mark was the young idealist, his blue eyes shining, his face revealing the excitement he felt about joining the older and well-known preachers. Because he was the youngest, John Mark probably carried their provisions: Jewish-baked cakes, dried cheese, pressed figs, a cruse of honey, and a gourd of soured goat's milk. Barnabas probably carried the manuscripts, parchment and papyrus of the Holy Books of Isaiah, Psalms and Daniel.

But the missionaries were not that well received in Perge. The Jews were skeptical, even suspicious of Paul. No doubt, his reputation as the arrogant Saul of Tarsus had preceded him. To add to that, he brought a strange message filled with dissension and unrest: their king – who was not really a king at all – had already come, he said. Their Messiah had been crucified by the Romans at the pleasure of the Jews in Jerusalem. His picture of the king of the Jews was hardly as a great conqueror like other kings in Persia or in Rome. The king of the Jews, Paul said, was an ordinary man, a carpenter from Nazareth, a nobody like a slave. When the local rabbi questioned him, Paul's answer was short.

The next day he probably set up his loom as a tent maker or a carpet weaver, work that was not only a means of financing his missionary travels but also his reason to move among the Gentiles, an excuse to be among the common people: soldiers, slaves, freemen and merchants, not to mention the made-up street women with high tiered hair, whores who openly solicited customers in the marketplace.

Although Paul was rebuffed by the Jews, his message no doubt appealed to the mixture of nationalities on the street, the pagans who stopped to talk, the Gentiles who listened to him preach. But when the local rabbi heard that Paul was eating with them, actually going to their homes, sitting at the tables and eating where Gentiles served unclean meat, he came one night to the place where the traveling preachers slept and brought a warning from the small orthodox Jewish community.

"You stray too far from the Torah," he must have warned. "The Jewish Law tells our people not to eat meat offered to idols, meat from blood and from things strangled. You know the Law. You stray too far away. The Law is clear." There was a long pause when no one spoke. John Mark turned away; Barnabas stood beside Paul as the rabbi said, "You cannot eat at their tables."

We can imagine that Paul's beady eyes glared back at the rabbi, his bushy eyebrows quivering. Scholars describe Paul as "sure and confident." Some say he was arrogant. He certainly made no effort to hide his anger. How dare another rabbi question him? He was free to preach his message, to make believers out of those who were not Jews. The elders in Jerusalem had agreed. The leaders of the church had agreed that he could convert the Gentiles.

John Mark closed the door. "He is right," the youngest preacher must have argued as the candles were burning low in the tiny room the men shared in a hostel near the synagogue. "We stray too far from the Law."

The deep voice of Barnabas agreed with Paul. "If our mission is to succeed," he said, "we must convert the masses."

"Accept the uncircumcised?" John Mark's question reflects the doubts and suspicion of many leaders in the Temple.

"Yes," Paul answered. "The easier way we leave for others. I have chosen the harder one."

John Mark was not convinced. It seems a safe bet that the youngest apostle didn't speak of it, but he knew all too well that Paul had never heard the rabbi from Nazareth, had never seen the Nazarene as he, John Mark, had seen Him in his own mother's house.

"The Law is clear: except ye be circumcised after the custom of Moses ye cannot be saved," John Mark repeated the old argument "Circumcision marks us as a chosen people; it sets us apart from the infidels, those who worship idols. The rituals have been handed down for generations and practiced all over the East."

Barnabas would have cried out, "John Mark, show respect. Who gives you the authority to question Paul?"

"Who gives us the right to preach a message different from the original?" John Mark certainly asked. "Surely our Lord intended the converts to follow the Law of Moses," he said, his anger rising.

"The God of Israel gives us the authority," Paul said. "And our Lord who said, 'There shall not be a corner of the world whither the name of the God of Israel and of the Messiah of Jacob shall not have reached.'"

John Mark grabbed his mantel and left the room. We are told that he "departed from them and returned to Jerusalem." Barnabas, too, would eventually leave the radical Paul and return to the Temple and the more orthodox factions. The record in Acts tells us that after the confrontation with John Mark, Paul fell ill in Perge, but the writer does not tell us what "thorn in the flesh" he suffered. Some scholars believe he contracted malaria on the coastal plains. The disease was prevalent and wide-spread. Other scholars believe Paul suffered throughout his life from an illness we call epilepsy.

Nineteen centuries later we found Perge in the middle of a corn field with stalks taller than I had ever seen back home. The site was discovered in the nineteenth century when a Turkish farmer plowed up a marble column. After that the vast city was excavated and today it stands in silence, miles away from the sea.

When we entered the site, we walked our separate ways – Susan to find the synagogue where Paul first preached, Steve to examine the architecture: the arches, the lintels, the Roman friezes and reliefs, workmanship long admired in the Western world.

I went to the baths where lizards run along the dry tiles, no more hot and cold running water. I walked down the wide colonnaded avenue of victors and climbed a narrow street to the houses, the remains of the living quarters, homes of the Gentiles who invited Paul to eat with them. In one small rectangular room I sat to brush the sand away on the steps. Underneath my feet was a blue and white mosaic floor in a carefully-laid geometric design, warm to touch in the midday sun.

Susan found me staring at the hundreds of thousands of ceramic pieces all in place after all the years.

"I'm trying to imagine who designed this pattern," I told her. We decided it was a Roman slave, an artist brought from Babylon.

We found Steve sitting in the rock-hewn stands in the largest stadium preserved from Roman times, two and one half times as long as a modern football field.

"I can hear it now," he said. "The chariots, the horses. Can you imagine the roar of the crowd?"

"Shh," Susan warned. "What's that?"

A John Deere tractor as shiny green and modern as any back home was making its way down the unpaved road behind the stadium. Behind it a horse-drawn wagon filled with Turkish farm women was heading home after a long day in the fields.

Twelve years after the first missionary journey, Paul visited Perge again, this time as a prisoner who had been condemned by the leaders in Jerusalem and put in prison because he preached a message different from the Law. In the fierce anger and controversy that surrounded the Temple, he had been dragged to the dreaded pit to be stoned but was saved at the last minute by friends and taken to safety in Caesarea. Since his first visit to Perge, he had crisscrossed the middle sea and the entire continent of Asia Minor. He had established churches in such faraway places as Ephesus,

Phillipi, Thessalonica and Corinth. He was sixty years old and on his way to Rome.

It's not hard to imagine that word had spread about his imprisonment and decision to stand trial in Rome. As a result, delegations awaited him at towns along the coast like Perge with gifts such as a mattress or a warm cloak that could double as cover during the night, and always another day's supply of kosher food.

Arriving on a small vessel called a trader, sometimes called a coaster and about the size our thirty-seven foot sailboat, Paul was a prisoner of the Italian centurion of the First Augustan Legion who had put his prisoners on the trader in the middle of August with hopes of transferring them to a passenger ship, a larger vessel farther to the west. No one wanted to get to Rome any more than Julius. He knew quite well that his chances of getting there increased as he moved around the coast.

Each night the trader pulled into port to deliver goods and take on passengers. No doubt Paul was allowed to go ashore and visit the little band of people who seemed to know him. Other prisoners weren't that lucky since they were probably members of robber bands that infested the highways of Judaea, those who were being sent to fight the wild beasts in the arena; they stayed chained to the bulkhead, forced to sleep with the animals below.

John Mark was right. The orthodox factions in the Temple in Jerusalem had formally accused the fiery Paul of preaching against the Jewish Law, the law of Moses. He couldn't deny that he had eaten at the table of the Gentiles and accepted uncircumcised heathens into the fold. Neither could he deny that he had generally created a new religion and spread it all over Asia Minor while the High Priest and his cabinet, the Sanhedrin, disputed the minutest details of ceremony.

The internal struggle for power, the battle between the Pharisees and the Sadducees, had reached indescribable gridlock, and Paul was caught up all the bitterness and animosity. Since he felt he was in the right, he was absolutely determined to take his message to the West and demanded his right to be tried in the Roman courts. After all, as his father and his grandfather had reminded him, he was Saul of Tarsus. He was born in no mean city.

6
Turkish Delights

Our weather was perfect. Mariners call them Halcyone Days, except, in our case, we were coasting in summer and real Halcyone Days come in winter, seven days before winter solstice and seven days after. Halcyone is the season of calm before and after the most dangerous winds of the Mediterranean. Halcyone floats undisturbed on the swells during those days. The Greek myth says she threw herself into the sea when her lover drowned in the unpredictable winds, and she was turned into a seabird that nests on the swells during Halcyone Days.

Around us the water was turquoise and so clear that entire cities could be seen beneath the boat; harbor towns that had been swallowed up by earthquakes lay on the sea bed. Marble columns, mosaic tile, and sea walls glistened through the shimmering water. Oceanographers once believed the sea was rising but now say the Mediterranean has risen no more than eighteen inches in five thousand years. Earthquakes have done the damage, they believe. The coast of Turkey is creasing, shifting, they say, because of the clash of tectonic plates.

According to our cruising guide, ahead of us on a peninsular was the abandoned city of Chima. It had long ago been trapped upriver by erosion. We used our binoculars to spot the fire above the city. The natural gas spews feebly now, but in ancient times the gas burst from the limestone rock and exploded in flames. The Greeks called it the Chimera, a terrible monster, part lion and part goat, its hind legs like those of a dragon, its breath a flame of fire.

In mythology it was Bellerophon who wrestled with the monster and conquered it. He sought the aid of Athena who gave him the golden bridle and led him to the spring on the mountain above us where Pegasus, the winged white horse, came to drink each morning. Bellerophon captured and mastered the powerful steed, mounted Pegasus and flew over the Chimera where he sent his arrows into the monster. Today most of the natural gas has escaped and the fire burns inconsistently, if at all.

On the other side of the peninsular, goatskin tents were set up under a vast orchard of gnarled olive trees. Modern nomads come down from the mountains for the summer months to live by the shore and cook over the open fire as their ancestors did. Year after year they pass the stories down to the next generation as they squat in Oriental fashion around their campfires.

There was always a surprise for us around the next bend. One morning on a rocky ledge above us, a Turkish farmer held his baggy britches high over his bare white knees. He stepped nimbly, as if he were dancing in slow motion.

"What's he doing?" I couldn't help whispering.

A woman in a long skirt and long-sleeved blouse, her kerchief tied securely around her head, came from her house and began scurrying about, moving clay jars below the ledge.

"Are they doing what I think they are doing?" I had an idea that the custom was ancient and well-known.

"I believe so." Steve agreed, grabbing the binoculars.

"Doing what?" Susan appeared suddenly from below.

"That's what they're doing," Steve assured us.

"Crushing grapes?" she asked.

"They're crushing all right, but they're crushing tomatoes." Steve could hardly believe his eyes.

"Tomatoes?" Susan took the binoculars.

We took turns watching the man crush mounds of vine-ripened tomatoes with his feet while the woman caught the juice that oozed, blood-red into the large clay jars. We were in that part of the world where they had tread grapes to make wine for thousands of years. They had crushed sage and turmeric for spices. They had pounded seed for flour since man first transplanted wild grains from the fertile coastal fields. Why not tomatoes? The Turkish farmer found his feet a handy tool for making tomato juice, even in the twentieth century.

Around another bend we motored close to intricately carved rock tombs, sarcophagi that stood marooned out in the water. They were once filled with treasure but are empty now, ravaged by pirates and thieves. The Lycians developed the tomb as an art form and buried vast riches with their dead. There on the coast they carved tombs, but high up in the mountains they cut grand temple facades in the face of red and yellow cliffs or carved twenty-ton depictions of cabins from stone. Such temple and house tombs reflect the grandeur of that ancient civilization. They had their own gods, their own language, and obviously a deep respect for their dead. That same civilization had a king named Midas who was fabulously rich but wished for more. We all know the story: when his wish came true, everything he touched turned to gold.

One afternoon we were stunned to see five little heads swimming out toward the boat, small boys gulping for air. One little fellow trailed the group, his black hair pasted to his tiny head as he paddled with one hand and held flowers in the other, a bouquet of purple and white bougainvillea held high over his head.

The wind was calm, we were hardly sailing, just floating, a good excuse to finish a chapter in the latest book or catch up with our journal writing. All that stopped when the boys scampered up the boarding ladder and stood at attention, dripping in their underwear, which they wore as swim wear, until Susan pointed to the cockpit seats, explaining that they had permission to sit even if their clothes were wet.

"Teacher," she said, pointing to me, but they didn't understand.

"Teacher," she repeated, grabbing a book from below, holding it in front of her and standing as if she were in the front of a classroom. She pointed toward me. "Teacher."

"Ah." They looked at me with wide black eyes.

"Gigek," the smallest fellow said, handing me the bougainvillea, the bouquet of flowers he had so carefully protected as he swam to the boat.

"Flowers. *Gigek.* Flowers," I responded in typical teacher fashion.

"Tabak," another fellow said, pointing to a plate.

"Plate. *Tabak*," I said. They smiled with new-found power: they were the teacher. I was the student.

"Kozluk." Glasses.

"Turbur." Binoculars. The language lesson continued while Susan went below to bake chocolate chip cookies.

"Terluk." Show. I showed them my flowers.

"Okumak." Read, the smallest fellow told me. He had delicate features and olive skin, the descendent of a vicier, I imagined, the ruling class during the Seljuk sultanate.

Sitting at the back of the group was a chunky fellow with a round face and slanting eyes who took the ballpoint pen from the cockpit table. He didn't think I saw him. I imagined his ancestors were the true Turks, the horsemen from Mongolia and the Golie Desert, the gazis, the warriors who rode out of the desert, taking booty as they spread Islam along the way.

A tall, thin fellow stood quietly, taller than the rest. For some reason, I imagined him to be Turkestani. But how could I tell? "Who is a Turk" is a question the Turks themselves can't answer. Modern Turkey is a conglomeration of ethnic groups from Arabia to the Balkans. In addition, the people along the Mediterranean coast have been introduced to the seafaring nations of the Western countries. Those young Turkish students sitting before me could have been descendents of Italians or Corsicans for all I knew.

Today Turkey is bound together, not by any one nationality but by one language, a new simplified Turkish language devised and taught to all citizens. Linguists say it's a purification of the complex Ottoman Turkish which was a mixture of Arabic, Persian and Turkish. The language is so new that the boys' parents had learned it in the village square when Mustafa Kemal, the founder of the Republic, traveled from village to village with chalk and a blackboard. He was a leader who knew that it takes more than uniforms and flags to bind a nation together; he believed only a common language can seal a national identity. The boys were proud to be teaching me their language.

I flunked the test while they ate chocolate chip cookies. The boys, of course, squealed with delight, but by that time Steve was getting antsy about Turkish fathers who might be waiting impatiently for their sons, so he put the boys in the dinghy and rowed them ashore. When he returned, the dinghy was filled with baskets of tomatoes and cucumbers –

and another bouquet of flowers, another armful of purple and white bougainvillea.

The best surprise was yet to come. Before the sun went down, another boat joined us in a quiet cove where we had anchored. It was a Turkish *gulet* (pronounced gou-lette), twice the size of RISE, a high rumped boat that reminded us of the PINTA, or the NINA or the SANTA MARIE, a boat that Columbus would have cherished. We watched it coming in and admired the highly varnished pine, with no corners, no joints, each plank turned and curved to perfection.

"Who owns a boat like that?" I asked.

"No one," Steve mumbled. "They're charter boats. Rented to oil rich Saudies."

"Or Kuwaites." Susan whispered.

There was a frantic display of anchoring – stern to, as sailors do in the Med, by dropping the anchor from the bow then securing the stern to the quay or in this case to the shore. After five attempts, the *gulet's* anchor held, much to our relief. The captain then took the heavy stern line between his teeth, dived in the water, and swam to shore. He tied the line to a tree.

"I hope it holds." I somehow couldn't trust the slender pine to secure such a vessel, but rather than sit and worry about our predicament next to a boat that could slew wildly into our home, I went below.

Steve and Susan followed and we rambled in the refrigerator for the last three Amstels. We clinked the bottles surreptitiously, having been reminded that we were still in Moslem country. The wail of Islam had come down from the mountainside five times that day, the chant sung by muezzins from the minarets: "There is no God but God, and Muhammad is the prophet of God." It's a song sung not to the glory of God but more like a warning that this life is serious business. The chant can stop frivolity in its tracks, bring a moment of relaxation to a halt – and ruin a bottle of beer.

But our cabin was cool. Soft lights reflected on the teak walls. We were content in our own company. This was, after all, Steve and Susan's home, complete with their small library, short wave radio, and global positioning system we could use if necessary. Except for the boat beside us tied to a pine tree, we felt secure.

Sailing in the Med was old-hat for Steve and Susan who had crossed the Atlantic to get there. All across the Atlantic Ocean, Susan continued aerobic exercises to the sounds of Tina Turner. Once in a storm, Steve lowered the sails, lashed the wheel, and came below to read *The Hunt for Red October*, interrupting the book occasionally to listen to the radio and send out his location to any vessel that might be on a collision course in the North Atlantic.

Three years before they had put careers on hold, his in architecture and hers in nursing education. They sold the house they had renovated in historic Charleston and moved aboard RISE. After the Atlantic, they crossed the English Channel then motored through the rivers and canals of France, planning to turn right, to sail to starboard and come home by way of Gibraltar, the Canary Islands, and the Caribbean. But when they reached Marseille, they were drawn like a magnet to the Italian coast, through the Greek islands, then to the Eastern Med. They sailed into the Black Sea, then south to Israel, wintering each year on the island of Cyprus.

That is where I joined them. The invitation was issued casually back home. They had flown home for Christmas, armed with photographs and charts of the Med which they spread out on the living room floor in front of the Christmas tree.

"There, Mom," Susan pointed to the spot on the floor usually reserved for my coffee table. "That's where you can meet us. You can sail along the coast of Turkey with us."

I protested. "You're sweet and thoughtful, but I don't want to intrude. Dad wouldn't have wanted me to do that." His sudden death that summer had unnerved me. I tried to pretend. I smiled a lot that Christmas, but inside there was a dark hole, a void. I remember walking from room to room, as if I were looking for a new self to be revealed behind the door.

"He wouldn't want you to be alone next summer. He'd want you to joins us when school's out." When Steve left the room, she whispered, "Steve wants you to join us."

I had overcome the empty nest syndrome. Our two daughters had married and moved away. Then Steve and Susan left to sail to distant lands. Their father and I had settled into a new and smaller house. We had worked to reinvent ourselves. It took months, years, and just as we felt confident with our new lives, a deadly cancer struck and I was alone.

"I don't want you or Steve, I don't want any of the family, to worry about me." What I really meant was "I need every one of you to pull me out of my loss. I've been sucked into grief. It's like quick sand and I can't get out. Don't you see how much I need you?"

Steve put his arms around me. "It's not that we're worried about you, Mom. We know how independent you are. It's just that we want you with us, especially for this leg of the trip."

I found them in a community of sailors representing nations from all around the world – like Lynn and Tom from Australia. She was a former headmistress. He was an engineer. They, too, had given up careers. They had built their own boat and spent two years crossing the Indian Ocean and motoring through the Red Sea.

We sat on their boat eating icy strawberry sorbet made with a portable ice cream machine attached to a wind generator.

"What more could one want from life?" Lynn, the headmistress-turned-sailor asked me. It was a rhetorical question, I thought, and didn't miss a spoonful.

"It's the bit of joy one adds to life oneself that really counts, isn't it?" she asked, looking me in the eye, this time forcing me to murmur, "Mmmm."

I nodded my head in agreement, but I didn't understand about taking responsibility for one's own happiness, not really, not then.

Most of us don't understand, but the sailor who wanders away from life's normal course and the land-lubber who marches to a different drummer understand. Most of us regard any detour along life's path as escapism. It's better to follow the safe and simple patterns, we think. We speak in condescending tones about "hippies" and "dropouts." We say those who wander "lack responsibility."

Yet, we who follow the narrow path find ourselves caught up in the maze of life, the labyrinth, the "rat race" we call it, and wonder why we are unhappy. It's hard to admit, even to ourselves, but secretly we suspect we have made the wrong choices. Where is the JOY? To overcome our dark suspicion, we pile on more work or rush through lunch. We change jobs or go back to school for another degree. Most of us feel sorrow, not joy, and wallow in the pain of our own misgivings.

The sailors I met had no such misgivings. They were assured by the simple wonder of a sunset or the sound of the sea – the pings, the gurgles, the splash of waves on the hull. Whether they were sailing the sea or rocking in a harbor, they were convinced they had found the Great Answer to the meaning of life.

Maybe they had.

A sudden pounding on the hull and we waited for disaster, sure the boat next to us had come loose, positive the gulet was slewing wildly before crashing into RISE.

Instead we heard voices and people speaking English. “Miami,” voices called out. “Are you American? What are you doing over here?”

Susan bound up the cockpit ladder, anxious to talk, to hear stories – to tell her own. She was obviously missing the companion-ship of others. Steve and I sat dumb-founded, finding it hard to believe Americans were in Kekova Sound.

But there they were, standing in a tiny rowboat waiting for an invitation to come aboard, offering us the gift of forbidden fruit, a bottle of wine, in the land of Islam

“Asking permission to come aboard the good ship RISE,” said the one in the group who assumed an affected military stance. Steve granted permission and they clamored up the ladder. They were members of an Elderhostel group, gray-headed grandmothers and grandfathers who had studied ancient history in Ephesus for a week, and after classes ended opted for an adventure to the coast.

Two were retirees from Boca Raton, Rita and Joe who wore matching outfits, white polyester slacks with purple and yellow striped sweaters. I couldn't decide if their wide-eyed look was a result of boredom or shock, as if somehow they had gotten on the wrong ship. They were dressed as if they were taking a cruise ship out of Miami. I couldn't imagine them enjoying the accommodations on a gulet, which had to be as basic as ours on RISE and that's pretty basic compared to Princess Line standards.

Katie from Portland, Oregon, climbed up our boarding ladder as if she were twenty-three, but she admitted to seventy. She had participated in thirty-five Elderhostels and traveled to eight foreign countries, she said, her eyes sparkling, her gray hair pulled to the top of her head in a glamorous bun. On her thin neck, her arms, and fingers she wore an array of American Indian silver.

"We're going to find the ancient city of Myra tomorrow," she announced. "You know Myra?" she asked.

Since no one else spoke, I said, "That's where Saint Paul boarded a ship to Rome."

"I've been telling her there's nothing there but a pile of rock," the woman sitting beside Katie said. It was Carol, her sister and traveling companion and far less adventuresome than Katie.

"If that's the way you feel," Katie told her, "I'll go see the pile of rock alone." Katie turned to me. "You want to go?" she asked. "Our captain says he knows a taxi driver who will take us."

David, the Elderhosteler who seemed to be the fount of all wisdom among the group, was eager to reveal what he had learned. He was telling Steve about ancient boat-building.

"*Gulet* is a bastardized version of the French word *goilette*," he explained. "It means schooner, but actually it's rigged like a ketch."

"I can't imagine keeping up the varnish," Steve said.

"Built out of pine. Nothing left on this coast but pine. They used all their hardwood centuries ago." David continued. "Shipbuilding was a major industry," he said. "The ancients used a variety of woods. A Roman shipbuilder could use fifty birch trees, three hundred oaks, and three hundred walnut trees to build one war galley."

"No wonder the hills are barren," Steve looked over and winked at me. We had seen nothing but rock, sculptured white limestone mountains and had read about the reasons for such erosion.

"After they felled the trees, the soil washed into the harbors and filled up the rivers," David explained. "Navigation to places like Myra became impossible. Entire cities were abandoned."

Joe from Boca Raton joined in. "It's easy to forget this is a Moslem country," he said, the reality of what he had learned sinking in. "People in the cities look Western."

"Of course they do," Rita, his wife said. "That's because they wear Western clothes." Her observation of any country never went deeper than the clothes worn by the natives.

"But you can feel it, that undercurrent of fundamentalism," Katie said, the grandmother who traveled to understand the cultures, to see more than the surface of a country. "The Turks may wear our jeans and tee-shirts but they don't trust us."

"There's plenty of anti-Western sentiment in the mountains near Syria," David said. "Our professor said traveling that far East on the coast would be dangerous."

"Maybe it's a good thing we didn't go to Tarsus," Susan whispered.

"They said large segments of society hold fast to the old traditions. Those people can be militant and openly hostile to any Westener," he warned.

We talked into the wee hours about the history of modern Turkey, the collapse of the Ottoman Empire, the formation of the National Republic under Ataturk and the separation of church and state.

"And the population doubles every thirty-four years," Katie added. "That's a continual problem, not to mention the problem of eight million Kurds who live in the southeast mountains."

The glazed look returned to Rita's and Joe's eyes. Carol slept through it all with her head resting on Katie's shoulder. Finally, we bid them goodnight.

The next morning, we piled into a battered, worn Mercedes driven by a Turk who looked as old as the car. Steve and Susan thought better of all this and decided to go snorkeling among the marble columns, harbor walls, and colorful mosaic floors. Off they went to get permission from authorities. So, six of us were left to go see Myra. The taxi driver nodded at Katie's instructions, assuring her that he knew where she wanted to go, the car careening around the mountainous curves, dust swirling through the open windows. Once I glanced back to see a cloud of limestone sand that marked our trail, the proverbial "Goodbye cruel world" ringing in my ear.

But the driver knew the way. Within an hour he turned onto Route 400 and pointed down to the other side of the hills, down to the plains around Demre Cay, ancient Myra, which is miles away from any sea.

Two thousand years after Paul, Myra is deserted except for a Byzantine church and in it the tomb of St. Nicholas, patron saint of sailors, whose bones have been removed and now rest somewhere in Italy. There is no sign of Paul, the earliest of all missionaries, who came there to board the Alexandrian grain boat. Neither is there any sign of the fragrant myrrh which came from a tree that has long since disappeared and was bottled and sold by Christian monks centuries later as a miracle cure. There are no ships, no relics to prove the story in Acts, not even a harbor, which was abandoned and silted up after the Romans left.

There is only the church and the patron saint of sailors that tourists, certainly American tourists, confuse with Santa Claus. The old city is, as Katie's sister warned us, "just a pile of rock."

With our curiosity satisfied, Katie showed the taxi driver a map and off we went in another direction, up another mountain until the road ended in a dusty parking area.

"Termessos," Katie said as we dismounted taking with us cameras, guide books, and bottled water. "It's the only city Alexander the Great failed to take."

An hour later we were climbing along a precipitous ledge. "I can understand why Alexander gave up on this place," I said, panting, out of breath, still scrambling over the rocks. We passed an aqueduct built long before before the Romans came along and caves that had been carved into the rock.

"This must be where they stored Nero's ice," David said under his breath.

"His what?" Rita asked, thinking he was putting her on.

"His ice," David said.

"What do you mean?" Carol wouldn't let go of that comment. "The Romans had no ice," Carol said.

"Of course they did. Nero ordered ice to be brought to his banquets."

"In fact he ordered ice sculptures." Katie knew her history.

"The Greeks had ice," David agreed.

"It came from mountain tops like this?" Rita asked, her curiosity piqued.

"Mountain tops like this," David explained. "Ice was buried deep in the rocks during winter and carried to Rome at any time of the year by swift relays of horses. Selling ice was big business around the civilized world. The ancients knew the good life."

"The aristocracy," I reminded them. "The few at the top of the social and economic ladder." I couldn't help thinking of the number of slaves needed to break up the ice and store the enormous chunks down inside the limestone rock.

Exhausted and out of breath, we sat to rest on rockhewn benches in a small theater overlooking the sea while Katie read from the guidebook.

"A hundred thousand people may have lived here once," she read. "They turned back Alexander's army. Then, for some unknown reason, the city was abandoned in the fifth century AD."

"Overrun by the local warlords from below," David guessed.

"Says here there's no evidence of a battle," Katie said.

"Disease," David ventured. "A plague that swept through the city."

"No evidence of Christianity," Katie added. "No early Christian symbols found here. Only Greek gods."

Sitting in the small Hellenistic theater overlooking the sea, we decided these people were no backward mountainous people who lived in poverty like Kentucky coal miners. These people were rich, not only in the amount of gold they mined, but in beauty and thought. These were the pure Greeks, the original immigrants to Asia Minor, the Ionians who fled the mainland and built the celebrated cities of the Xanthos valley: Tlos, Pinara, and Xanthos itself. These Greeks performed great plays on the stage below us, and I wondered which play? Had the tragedy been played out on the stage or in the ancient ruins that surrounded us?

On the way back to Kekova Sound, there were more surprises. We passed a wagon weighted down with freshly-cut sheaves of wheat and pulled by a mountain man, gnarled and aged and toothless. On the other side of the road, there was a modern Coca Cola plant under construction and across the highway hundreds of brand new John Deere Tractors for sale.

"This is what I like about Turkey," Katie whispered. "The countryside is filled with contradictions, the old and the new side by side."

That night we returned their visit. We went aboard their charted Turkish gulet. Steve admired the workmanship of the balustraded pine, I sipped more Greek wine, and we all ate the spicy hor d'oeuvres the captain's Turkish wife spread out before us. It would be our farewell meal. The next day we'd be moving on to begin our final trek through the Greek islands. We'd wait for the right winds, Steve explained, just as the Alexandrian grain boat waited, then we'd hop from island to island, always in sight of land, until we spotted Crete, our destination since we were following Paul's course to Rome, ill-fated as it was . . . .

"How did they know which way to go back then?" Joe from Boca Raton wondered. "How did they know where Rome was?"

"They probably navigated using the length of the day," Steve explained. "Something like, 'Sail for ten hours keeping the island shaped like a dragon to port.' They thought in terms of an average day's run."

"And they handed down stories, their sailing directions," Susan said. "They sailed from memory."

"If they forgot the stories, they got lost." Steve said.

"They'd never get to Rome," someone said.

"Exactly. It was practical to keep in sight of land," Steve went on. "They used the position of the sun and the stars for long distances. Even the Vikings sailed along a coastline. It was in cloudy weather that navigation became bewildering. It still is."

"You crossed the Atlantic. How did you prepare for that?"

"Other sailors," Steve admitted. "The talk of the sea is as important as it ever was. When sailors came into Charleston from a long sail, I made it a point to talk to them, hear their stories, learn from their experience."

"But word of mouth is not that accurate. You had back-up systems, communication systems that the ancients never dreamed of." David was not that convinced.

"Put that way, I would agree with you," Steve said, "but you must remember that if you never had a clock or a compass, if you had spent your life at sea, your sensory perception of time and direction would be sharper, much more so than ours. A man who lives on the sea for any time at all knows his direction. If he can see the North star, direction is a piece of cake."

Katie agreed. "You're right. We grew up on the west coast. When I was a child, old fishermen used to say they could tell all they needed to know by looking at the sea birds. Our father used to tell us about a sailor who could never do the mathematics to work out his longitude so he sailed using the five L's – Latitude. Lead. Log. Look-out and trust in the Lord. The five L's of navigation."

"If you note the relationship between wind direction and the sea each time you have a glimpse of the sun, you can make a good guess at your heading even if the sky is overcast," Steve said, "and you know when the wind changes and how much because it takes a few hours for the sea to follow it. By the time the sea comes round, you have a new relationship of ship to wind direction and you start observing all over again. Remember that the ancients knew the water and they had been doing this all their lives."

So the talk rambled on our last night in Turkey. As we thought about it, we decided that the more sophisticated we become, the more high-tech we become as a result of more and more computerized navigational aids, the more we lose our own sensory perception, our capacity to make deductions, our ability to think and to reason.

"I guess we're spoiled because we have charts and state-of-the-art navigational equipment," Steve said, but there was a look of affection when he glanced below at his nav station.

It was Katie who had the last word. "A chart wouldn't have done the ancient mariners much good. They couldn't read."

When Julius the Centurion passed through with his prisoner, the city called Myra was still a bustling harbor town where ships from around the middle sea came to take on fresh crew. Large ships scheduled for long crossings came to hire experienced pilots. Shipyards were busy hauling vessels, refitting the riggings and patching sails. The air was filled with the planing of timbers and the stench of filthy bilges; the smell of cattle and sour grain filled the air, along with putrescent meat and fish that mingled with the rancid odors of oil and vinegar.

The centurion's hunch was right. Waiting in the harbor when Julius and his prisoners arrived by coaster, was a large ship scheduled to leave for Rome, its hold filled with corn and grain. The ship had been conscripted into the imperial mercantile fleet in Alexandria with orders to sail to Rome. The passenger list was filled; there was barely enough room for the crew, certainly not a group of prisoners, but Julius quickly recognized the opportunity and as centurion of the Augustan Guard threw his weight around, not to mention a few gold ducets; thus, the group was guaranteed a place on the passenger list. Paul was assigned a bunk next to Julius who had stopped chaining Paul to his wrist, not even to his bunk, but he kept the trouble-making Judaean near him, just in case.

The ship was both a commercial and pleasure craft. Unknown to Roman naval authorities, the captain had picked up passengers along the way, some who thought they were taking advantage of the off-season rates but were really paying outrageous prices "under the table." Most were entertainers, eager to get to Rome for tryouts, the possibility of joining the court of Nero Claudius Caesar Augustus Germanicus who would become a bride in the next few months. He, that is, she (the most royal of Roman transvestites) would put on the veil of a virgin and go through a long and complicated ceremony to accept the blessing of Apollo and Aphrodite and become a bride. Afterward there would be weeks of festivities, night after night of celebration for the council of ministers, the commandant of the Practorian Guard, the elite Augustan Guard, and the highest military figures in Rome.

On board, waiting for their chance to perform at the festivals were musicians, flute players, harpists, cymbal players, psaltery player, lutist, all with their instruments.

There were Egyptian dancing girls, actors, comedians, mimes, many of them famous in the provinces, all sailing to Rome to seek their fortune.

One passenger who was being given special treatment was noticeably not an entertainer; nevertheless, he was assigned a berth near the military quarters. He was Talamus, the hairdresser who became famous when he gave Caesar his new look, the girlish ringlets that encircled his full, fleshy face. Talamus stayed to himself and seemed withdrawn and nervous, as if he were worried about what he might find when he got to Rome. If Nero were in his manly mood, he wouldn't like the curls and Talamus would be in trouble, for he knew how difficult it was to suggest masculinity about Nero's smooth, oily skin, and his full lips.

Below in chains were the prisoners from the provinces already condemned to fight the wild animals, their chains attached to the bulkhead of the ship itself. Although the ship captain had managed to leave Alexandria without cages of wild animals, there were wooden boxes of pheasants for the banquets and barrels of African game fish. There were crates of Cilician pomegranates and figs, Cypriot wine, Asian perfumes, and Judaean oils, all of which had to arrive in Rome before the wedding feast.

No doubt Paul was concerned about making the passage across the sea so late in the season. He knew about the winds that come on so late in the summer, the sudden winds that whip down the mountains, funnel on the plains, gather speed and charge across the coastal water, surprising ships, challenging the most experienced crew, and terrifying passengers. But he busied himself by getting acquainted with the travelers and especially the sailors. An old and experienced traveler by sea as well as by land, Paul could speak more like a sailor than a traveler, so he went around to the crew of the ship, talking with the sailing master, the anchorers, the men in charge of the sails and even the overseer of the ship's slaves. In the evenings when he sat down with the converts to the new religion for their common meal, some of the crew members joined him, this strange man who stood on deck far into the night praying to his invisible God.

No doubt the captain, too, was concerned about the course he would take for a voyage so late in the season. If the winds held out, he would cross the Aegean to the island of Rhodes or perhaps the island of Kos, well-known as the birthplace of the renowned Hippocrates. However, his passengers would have preferred lively Rhodes even though the colossus that spanned the harbor had fallen victim to an earthquake and lay at the bottom of the sea. After the stop at one of those islands, he'd island hop to Crete, then to Cythera, and then sail around the boot to Rome. Of course, he had talked to the Asian weather pundits, but what did they know? He had listened to the local sea lore and could remember the stories that might be important in case of early fall winds. He probably reasoned that he had no real worries because in Myra he had hired a sailing master with impeccable credentials as a pilot.

He felt as we did: he sailed in the unseen company of countless sailors who had passed safely over those waters for centuries. His knowledge of the past gave him confidence. Any sea captain in the first century knew he was sailing well-traveled waters. Even though he had never heard of a chart or a compass, even though he could never in his wildest imagination consider a computerized print-out of a weather forecast ten days in advance, he was sure he could make it to Rome. Others had crossed from Alexandria, Tyre, or Sidon this late in the season. Why wouldn't he be able to do the same?

7
In the Mirror

As we crossed from the continent of Asia Minor to the island of Rhodes, I sat on the deck wedged in between all the cruising necessities lashed down for another overnight voyage: two sets of oars, the ladder, five jerry cans of extra diesel fuel, three cans of extra water, extra jib sheets, extra lines, and our all-purpose bucket we could use for bailing out the bilge in an emergency, heaven forbid. By midnight the winds had picked up and shifted to come at us on the nose, however, and before long RISE was rolling and tossing. The currents were so confused that Steve lowered the jib, reefed the mainsail and resorted to using engine power. Even with our sixty-five horsepower Perkins at full RPM's, we were making little headway toward Greece.

Susan turned pale, mumbled something between her cupped hands, and dashed to the side of the boat. After losing her supper to the sea, she stumbled below and collapsed on the settee. I grabbed the wheel.

"Keep her up, Mom," Steve shouted from the nav station where he was studying the chart to find an island, a place to escape the worst of the wind. "Point her up." The radio crackled as he tuned in for a weather report. "More, Mom. Up. Point her up. Point her up."

The *meltemi* is only one of the winds that blasts across the Mediterranean with no warning and sends small boats like ours, large ones too, scurrying for safety. There's also the *levanter*, the *mistral*, the *boro*, and the *sirocco*. Then there's the Greek *gregale*, a wind so feared by ancient mariners that war galleys were pulled out of the water by November 15 and put in dry dock for safekeeping.

It was the wrath of the wind that kept Odysseus from rounding the island of Cythera and drove him away from his Greek shores. He lost all hope of reaching Ithaca after the Trojan War: " . . . . for nine days I was driven by those cursed winds across the fish-infested sea," he lamented as he saw his homeland fade in the distance, and so began the seventeen-year sailing adventure that Homer recorded in the fifth century BC.

According to Roman records, after the seas closed, harbor towns were overrun with galley oarsmen out of work until spring when the seas opened again.

During the Middle Ages, towns like Pisa and Genoa continued the ancient maritime codes that forbade shipping during the dangerous winter months. In spite of all the precautions, however, maritime records are filled with evidence of shipwrecks caused by the winds of the Mediterranean. As late as the seventeenth century thirty-eight Barbarosso galleys were driven onto the coast of the Adriatic where they broke up in the raging seas. An entire fleet of Spanish galleys was lost that same century returning too late in the sailing season. The sea is a graveyard of ships, a field of excavation for marine archaeologists.

To the ancients the king of the winds, Aeolus, confined the winds in a cave, letting them out as needed with help from his four wind gods: Boreas, the North Wind; Zehpyrus, the West Wind; Notus, the South Wind; and Eurus, the East Wind.

What Aeolus sent us the night we left the Turkish coast was no mild zepher. It was a full-fledged North Wind, a *meltemi,* they call it. We found an island and anchored in spite of the wind, which was relentless in its fury, hell-bent on snatching us in its fangs, slinging us from beam to beam and rolling us from side to side. Once during that first night there was a sudden, deafening quiet, but the wind gods were playing a trick. Just when we thought the storm had passed, Aeolus unleashed fresh wind with renewed force and a fearful sound. For three nights we slept fitfully, if at all. The anchor rode, thirty feet of stainless steel chain, dragged endlessly on the rocky sea bed beneath us, its constant movement sending up echoes in the night like ghosts stalking in their watery graves.

Susan lay lifeless on the settee, unable to move. Steve sat like stone at the nav station, staring at the chart before him, listening to the radio beside him. I mentally counted the days until school started, but my unit in Greek mythology was losing its appeal.

"How long does a *meltemi* last?" I asked, giving up hope that I would ever see the island of Crete, my dreams dashed like the myth born there, the story of Icarus who flew too close to the sun and fell into the sea.

"I dunno," Steve said, getting up from his place at the nav station slowly and peering through the port holes. The water was seething around us. "Two, three more days," he said, shaking his head.

"A week." Susan's voice sounded weak. "It could last a week, Steve. Then what do we do?"

"We've never been held up a week, hon." Steve said, consoling her, moving to the settee to pat her forehead and rub her listless arm He recognized her malady, the age old half-autistic state brought about by the monotony of bad weather and nausea. Even hearty sea captains fall prey to its debilitating effects. Single-handed boats have been known to flounder in the seas, lose round-the-world races because of it; sailors, alone and seasick, fall victim to self-pity and mental anguish. Some have been known to hear voices or see a mirage before they recover from the malaise. Sailors hallucinate and walk away from their ships into the sea. When Odysseus heard the seductive sounds of the Sirens, he forced his crew to tie him to the mast. Boats are found floating at sea without their captains, with no evidence of foul play. Joshua Slocum, the first sailor to circumnavigate the globe single-handed, heard whispers in the night but lived to tell about it.

If Susan's energy faded, mine increased. My urge to be "mother" returned with a vengeance. Now was the time for any good mother to come to the aid of her children, was it not?

"We ought to eat a good meal," I announced. Susan moaned. Steve eyes rolled back into his head.

"That's what we need. Food. Energy." I looked in the galley. The boat was a wreck. Everything was out of place, tossed from the galley to the table to the bunks. The oriental rugs were scrunched thoughtlessly in the corners; the cabin floor was a minefield of boat shoes, books, and canned goods. I had made the mistake of opening a cabinet door and as I did, the boat rolled to port, the cabinet door swung open, and all our can goods tumbled out; cans of peas, tuna, Campbell's chicken noodle soup, Crisco, and Cheese Whiz rolled onto the cabin sole. Every time the boat moved, more cans rolled from under the bunks and spun around on the floor.

"Pasta with a mild tomato sauce," I said, determined to get the crew back on its feet. Susan turned her face to the blank wall, the bulkhead. Steve returned to his cave at the chart table.

"We don't need food, Mom," Susan said, her voice as if coming from a sick bed.

"Sure we do," I insisted. "We'll all feel better." I purposely put a lilt in my voice.

"It's not food that we need," she insisted.

"Susan." Steve spoke sternly in the direction of the sick bed. Then turning to me, he said calmly, "She just needs peace and quiet, Mom, until the weather . . ."

"But son . . . ," I interrupted in my softest, most motherly voice. "We all need to eat. We need energy."

"Then eat a peanut butter sandwich," Susan said, regaining enough energy to respond.

"Something hot," I said, "Something filling." I was not to be diverted from my mission to play the role of mother.

Suddenly Susan rose from her bunk as if from the dead, her sheet wrapped around her like a shroud. She stumbled to the galley and reached for the two sauce pans on the burners, one for pasta, one for sauce. Grabbing the pans and raising the utensils over her head, she stood to protect her territory, shouting, "It's my kitchen. It's my kitchen."

Steve shot up from the nav table, took one giant step across the cabin, and grabbed the heavy aluminum utensils from her hands, prying her fingers open, "Come on, Sue. Get hold of yourself." His voice was calm but commanding.

"It's my kitchen." She was hysterical. The walls of the small boat were closing in on her; the old malady called seasickness was draining her emotionally.

"It's my kitchen. Nobody cooks in my kitchen," she cried, stumbling through the cabin, and into the forward cabin, slamming the door that separated the areas. For a long time we could hear the muffled sound of sobs. Steve stood staring at the door in bewilderment, her sauce pans dangling by his side.

We had lived for weeks in a space no wider than your typical walk-in closet, no longer than a cubicle and only as high as the average reader is tall. RISE has a beam of twelve feet three inches; that is, it is as wide as the average car is long. This particular boat had headroom of six feet, but when storage space and lockers are built into that space, the actual living area is reduced considerably. After living in a tiny, closed-in space, we didn't need a psychologist to tell us that Susan's coping responses had shut down, that the constant invasion of her personal space was taking its toll and causing her undue stress. In other words, she had "had it."

In the silence that followed, Steve and I ate peanut butter sandwiches and listened to BBC on the short wave radio. Even hearing about the death of the Ayatoallh Ruhollah Khomeini, leader of the militant fundamentalists in Iran, didn't take our minds off our misery.

The island that protected us looked like all others in the Med, limestone rock pushed up from the core of the earth when Africa and Europe collided twenty-million years ago. During that tumultuous clash of tectonic plates, the earth shook, Africa moved north, and the water between the continents was closed off from the Atlantic to the west and from the Red Sea to the east. For millions of years, the area we know as the Mediterranean looked something like the Dead Sea. Its water evaporated.

Then five and one-half million years ago at the western end, where the two continents were fused, the Atlantic Ocean suddenly and inexplicably roared through, filled the dry basin and separated the two continents again. The massive flood reduced tall mountains to islands and buried a vast land to make the Mediterranean, called the middle sea during ancient times. After the deluge, islands like tiny Kastelorizo was all that remained of a limestone mountain. The trees are gone now. Only brown grasses grow where sheep and goats roamed for centuries. Fine sand swirls in the wind, for the fertile top soil was washed down into the sea long ago. The island that protected us from the *meltemi* was the smallest of the Dodecanese Chain and only four nautical miles from the Turkish coast.

The next morning when the *meltemi* died down, I jumped ship. Susan was still nauseated. Steve was coiling the lines, checking to see what damage the wind had done on deck. Soft music was coming from the stereo as I puttered off toward shore. I tied the dinghy up to the nearest tree, followed a goat path, and walked along the spiny ridge of the island until I saw a town nestled on the other side, a cluster of whitewashed houses surrounding a natural harbor. Blue caiques bowed and dipped in swells left over from the storm. Mounds of yellow net were piled on the quay.

Passing by a chapel at the edge of the town, I peeked in the window. Elaborate gold and brass icons sparkled beneath the central gold leaf dome. I closed my eyes and held my breath when I saw something move. An imposing figure stared back at me. A large gold cross hung loose over his black vestment, a priest with a black beard and a high black mitre who nodded kindly when he realized he had startled me. He motioned me to come in, but I left hurridly. His was a presence that exuded power, a black magic, perhaps something almost supernatural. It was a presence that had preserved the Eastern church for centuries, even though the land of Islam was only three miles away. The island had been invaded by the Turks, the Venetians, and the Crusaders, but its Greek Orthodoxy was stronger than ever.

At an outdoor cafe near the harbor, a woman my age with a British accent asked me to join her for lunch. We had smiled at each other, recognizing our mutual Anglo Saxon heritage and our similarities in age. It was our hair: dirty blonde with a sprinkling of grand-motherly gray.

"We sail here every year, my husband and I," she explained. "It's quite crowded in Rhodes, you know. We came early to get away from the storm," she explained. Her husband was back on their boat repairing a damaged bowsprit.

I told her about our sleepless nights on the exposed side of the island. Remembering Susan's malady, I thought it was too bad we didn't find this protected harbor.

"Americans rarely see islands like these. Not much tourism here. Not much of anything. Fishermen here barely make a living. Too deep. No shallow shelves where marine life can thrive. No long distance fishing fleets here. Only one-family operations. Most of the young people leave to go to Athens for jobs," she explained, the woman with pictures of seven grandchildren she showed me proudly.

During lunch we were distracted by gregarious Greek fishermen at the table next to us, raising their wine glasses in a toast. They pushed their chairs back noisily and stood, their glasses clinking ceremoniously. They turned and shouted something in Greek. They looked toward the quay, but no boat was coming in that we could see.

Instead, a handsome young Greek came striding down the quay, a "hulk," my students would have called him, a thin Greek wearing skintight jeans and a loose-fitting sweater who shuffled his shoes along the concrete and cocked his head back, his shoulder-length black hair flowing behind him.

He made me think of Homer's line: "A stripling in the first flush of manhood." That's the way the poet described a young Greek god. This stripling, too, was "straight and swift and strong," and I was sure this one was the likes of Dionysus himself.

"Watch this," the British woman warned, as if she had seen this before.

The fishermen jeered good-naturedly. They called and whistled, but the young man ignored them and strutted down the quay. They heckled, their voices louder, but he turned away and cocked his head, as sure of himself as the god who was adored by all the girls in ancient Greece.

When the fishermen heckled again, the young Greek stopped. He thrust his shoulders back and bent his head ever so slightly, nodding, acknowledging their compliment. There was a round of applause at the table and another toast as the young Greek turned and walked swiftly down a narrow cobblestone street.

"The town Casanova," the British wife guessed.

"The local stud," I decided but said nothing.

The chief of revelry, we both supposed. I looked at the other woman and saw myself. I saw the gray in her hair and sighed. Oh, to be young again. She, too, had a vaguely sad look in her eye. Oh, to follow a Dionysus, to be like the maenads, dancing with our heads thrown back, our hair disheveled, our hearts burning with desire. But the years fly past and one day you look in the mirror and see yourself as the aging woman you never meant to become – or you watch a "stripling in the first flush of manhood" – and you wonder where all the time has gone.

The British woman said goodbye and went back to her husband; the fishermen dispersed, and the shops along the waterfront closed their doors. It was siesta time, and behind the restaurant where I sat alone, there were muffled sounds in the kitchen: the movement of an iron skillet or a chair sliding across a stone floor.

I strolled to the Turkish section of Kastelerizo, where a small mosque stood back from the harbor. It was vacant now: the Turks were gone, their houses boarded up and abandoned, burned and gutted from a fire perhaps. Puzzled, I walked back to the Greek section, where the houses had been restored, where colorful blue and green shutters hung at the windows. Highly-varnished oak doors looked so inviting that I stopped in front of one house to rest under its stafalia, its grape arbor.

When a woman appeared at the door, I apologized, but she wouldn't hear of my leaving and insisted that I rest there. She needed to sit, too, and feel the cool wind against her face. She lifted the skirt of her apron to fan her perspiring forehead, this Greek woman whose name was Sophia, if I understood correctly. She did not smile easily, this woman whose Greek Orthodox mother and grandmother, whose long ancestry had been warned to leave the island, to give the land up to the Turks, or the Venetians or the Germans.

"A kitchen gets hot on a summer day," she must have said. I agreed, nodding my head and using my hand as a fan. "And I must cook every day for six, seven, sometimes ten people," she explained, using her fingers to show me the numbers.

"Ah, that's hot work," I lamented. She agreed, taking off her apron and pulling the fabric of her loose housedress away from her moist skin.

"Beautiful flowers," I said, pointing to the flower pots that lined the walkway into the tiny courtyard beside her house filled with red geranium, begonia, enormous elephant ear plants, oleander and purple bougainvillea.

"But I don't have time to take care of my flowers as I should," she must have said, "and then the *meltemi* comes. Look. All my beautiful flower pots along this wall crashed." She stood to show me how they fell, her flowers ruined, her handsome urns smashed.

"Meltemi," she said, shaking her head and making a "Tsh, tsh" sound with her teeth.

"Ah, yes, the *meltemi.*" I agreed that *meltemi* winds could cause havoc.

She guessed I was German.

No.

English?

No. American. Our boat lay at anchor across the island.

Using my Greek dictionary, we communicated, but with great difficulty, for she spoke in the unbroken tradition of the Greek language. Her language was more Greek than the people who lived in Athens; she was more Greek than the Greek women there. Her isolation had kept her traditions more Greek than those on the mainland. Women like her had held her people together through hordes of invaders. They had refused to leave their church, their island, their home. Like women on islands across the Mediterranean, Sophia had stood fast and shouted, "I am Greek. This island is Greek. This is my home." And when the foreigners left, her Greek traditions, her religion, and her language were stronger than ever. Under the very nose of the Ottoman masters, the Greeks preserved their language, their village life and their rituals. The Eastern Church flourished in spite of Islam and through it all, offered magnificent rituals to lift their spirits, a magic that protected them from the infidels.

An old woman dressed in black joined Sophia and me, her mother, wearing her black kerchief, black dress and black hose. She shuffled toward us across the cobblestone street dragging her feet, her black shoes worn down at the heels. We couldn't communicate, but we sat and smiled. Somewhere a bucket was lowered into a cistern and inside Sophia's house a baby cried.

"Please. Come," Sophia said. Even in Greek that was easy enough to understand. She lead me through the small courtyard and into her dark, cool living room. Her handiwork was everywhere. Like the Byzantine women who had come before her, she knew instinctively that she must decorate richly to give life meaning. She must add decency to her home even if her island was doomed to invasion after invasion. Her screenless windows were curtained with hand-crocheted lace. Her pillows were encased in matching hand-crocheted covers. Hand-embroidered religious tapestries hung on the walls.

"Who is that?" I pointed to the photograph among the tapestries, a picture of a dark-haired beauty. It was her daughter, the only girl in the family, who lived in Athena, as far away to Sophia as America seemed to me at that moment. The daughter was the only child who had left the island. Four boys lived at home, she said, fishermen like their father, one with a wife and baby, Sophia spoke quietly, fingering the smooth glass over the photograph as if stroking her daughter's dark hair.

"I know you miss her," I told her. "She's beautiful." I stroked the glass with her and told her how I, too, missed my daughters when they married and left home, how I missed their perfume, their laughter, their muffled sounds in their room. She held me close and thanked me for caring.

Another picture on the wall captured my attention. It was a photograph of Kastelorizo in the nineteen thirties when the island was obviously rich and fashionable, a resort for rich Europeans, no doubt. In the picture Parisian ladies paraded along the quay. Hydroplanes sat tied up in the harbor after a safe landing. The waterfront shops looked prosperous. Elegant houses reached to the top of the hillside.

What happened to the houses on the hill, I asked. What caused the fire? The War, she told me. Something about the War, something about the Allies in the Second World War, but I couldn't understand.

I would learn later about the shifting alliances on the Greek islands caught between Europe and North Africa. I would learn that most of the Dodecanese islands fell in line with the Germans by supplying landing strips and burying giant fuel tanks to refuel the Luftwafe. As a result, the Allies devastated the island with air strikes and bombing raids which turned the mountain into a burning inferno. After the war only three hundred residents returned to begin life on the island again.

It was late when I walked back across the mountain and heard sawing and hammering in one of the gutted house. After all the years, islanders were still returning, determined to cling to what was left of the life on the mountain. People around the middle sea have been returning and rebuilding for centuries. They learned long ago to wait, be patient, and, most of all, practice self-sufficiency. In times of drought or famine they patiently mended walls and cast artillery. In times of peace they rebuilt the fortifications for they knew, above all else, there would always be another king who would invade the island. There would be another pirate ship to steal the grain reserves. There would be another marauder who would take over for a mere show of power.

As I reached the boat, I smelled chocolate chip cookies and knew Susan was well again. She had overcome the old malady that hits hard when the winds get rough and the living gets close.

"We've been waiting for you, Mom. A British couple stopped by earlier to tell us about the grotto. Let's go see it before it gets dark. They said it's not to be missed." She handed me the first cookie to come out of the oven. "I'm sorry, Mom," she said. "I apologize for last night. I don't usually . . ."

"There's nothing to apologize for," I said, accepting the cookie, still soft and warm and gooey. "It's over." I said, my taste buds ready for chocolate. "We won't mention it again."

We haven't.

Around each headland, we checked for an entrance to the underwater cave. Steve mistook the purple mountain shadows for an opening. I thought a place in the undergrowth looked like an archway. At last Susan spotted the entrance.

"That's it," Steve agreed and waved us down in the dinghy, telling us to lie flat on the floor. "Don't move," he yelled as he revved the motor and took us through the entrance, the rubber raft squeezing through with only inches to spare over our heads.

The late afternoon sunlight blasted through the opening with us, making the clear blue water shimmer beneath us, turning the vaulted ceiling turquoise, mauve, and emerald. The sight was so spectacular, the silence so overwhelmingly pronounced that my heart pounded, and I held my breath. The world outside sounded distant, remote, ethereal.

Perhaps we had transcended time and space, I thought. Was the grotto real? Perhaps I was having some "other world" or "outer body" experience. For a fleeting second I closed my eyes, but I knew the grotto was real. I knew much more than that. I knew another woman had seen the grotto, a woman of another civilization had seen it when wild grains grew on the hillsides and green trees covered the mountain. She, too, felt regret at the passing of time. She, too, remembered when she followed the god to the mountain and danced with her head thrown back. She felt the link between the past, the present, and the future. In that instant, I understood the continuity. In that underwater cave, cathedral-like in its splendor, a secret place so insignificant it was ignored by the rest of the world, I felt the link. I felt the connection between civilizations. I grasped the truth, simple as that truth is: that we all dream the same dreams and feel the same losses. I felt the stream as I had never felt it before and knew without any doubt that all else – religions and emperors, temples and treasures – all else fades in its power.

8
A Man for the Season

If we had too much wind leaving Turkey, the Alexandrian grain boat leaving Myra in 57 AD had too little. In fact, for days they could find no wind at all - zilch, none - so there the boat sat with flat seas and 276 restless passengers who were not in the least happy about the living conditions on a hot, crowded, smelly grain boat. To stave off mutiny, the captain ordered the crew to pull the ship along using the long boat, a slim row boat used for short trips to shore and for pulling a heavy grain boat along when there was no wind. A grain boat, by the way, is a large thick-waisted clumsy vessel, not to be confused with a thin war galley or a swift pirate ship with three banks of oarsmen.

Tensions on board must have been unbearable, but we know few facts about the voyage because the captain left no log, no written record. It is doubtful that he could write; in fact, few ancient mariners could write. What we know about the trip has been handed down in Acts, the biblical account written, scholars believe, by an educated Greek called Luke who accompanied Paul on this ill-fated voyage. The writer, whoever he was, must have been stricken with the old malady called seasickness or perhaps he was disgusted with the deplorable conditions, for he recorded only that " . . . we made slow headway for many days and had difficulty arriving off Knidos."

Knidos, we know, lay at the western tip of the coast and was known for its theaters and temples, the most prominent of these was poised on a bluff overlooking the harbor and visible far out to sea. It housed the most celebrated nude statue of Aphrodite on the mainland. No doubt the heathen passengers went ashore to pay their respects and buy souvenirs. While they were gone, the crew put the animals on shore and washed down the boat. Presumably Paul preached more fervently than ever under the shadow of the love goddess.

Although there was no wind, thus no means of moving the ship, the captain must have had a plan. Here was the beginning of the Aegean, where a ship could slide with the current all the way down to the island of Crete. No doubt he planned to do just that and land on the north shore. There he'd wait for favorable winds, then sail to Cythera. He'd be home free then. As all the ancients before him had done at Cythera, he'd pick up wind from the south, a strong wind from Africa that would take the ship all the way to Rome.

There could be one hitch in the plan to slide with the current. He could miss the island of Crete altogether, and if that happened, he'd be forced to sail back up from Africa where he'd be caught on Crete's south shore, and everyone knew the stories about the dangers along that shore. Those stories had been handed down for centuries. Even the Romans avoided the craggy southern shore of Crete.

After only a few days at sea, the captain knew he was in trouble. The realization came as no shock, but to say he was disappointed would be putting it mildly. His vessel had been conscripted into royal service when he declared his cargo of seventeen tons of grain; and although the Romans paid handsomely, he subscribed to the usual arrangement of merchant ships going to Rome from the provinces. That is, in ports along the way he could take on passengers and demand gold ducets, cash under the table, so to speak. Then along came Julius, with whom he worked out another lucrative contract by taking on the prisoners, who were no trouble at all. He stood to make a grand profit on the black market.

After the slow, windless sail that must have been like floating down a river, the twin peaks of Mount Ada and Mount Ditka appeared suddenly in the clouds. Unfortunately, the mountains were to starboard, to his right. His ship had passed by Crete. He must have been concerned about the danger south of the island: the perilous white squalls that hurl down the craggy mountain tops with no warning, the force of nature that turns the Cretan Sea into fume before a ship knows what hit it.

Thinking through the situation, the captain commanded the sailing master to skirt the southern shore. There were alternatives; that is, he could take one of two courses of action. He could play it safe and slip quietly into the first anchorage he saw, as remote and uninhabitable as it might be. On the other hand, he could keep going, say nothing, pick up the winds, and cross the gulf to a friendlier spot: a harbor town on the other side of the island with Cretan wine and Cretan women, no doubt a more desirable place to spend a winter.

The captain could not have pondered long over his decision. He didn't have the luxury of time, and with a high ranking Roman officer on board, he put the question to Julius. If anything happened to the cargo, it would be better to have an officer on his side. But Julius thought there should be a meeting; he thought they should discuss the situation with the sailing master and with the prisoner who had done a great deal of sailing around the middle sea and may, after all, have some kind of contact with the invisible God he prayed to night after night.

At the meeting Paul had no trouble speaking his mind. "Sirs," he said, "I perceive that the voyage is likely to be accompanied with hardship and much loss, not merely to ship and cargo, but also to our lives." He, too, had heard about the unpredictable winds, the dangerous squalls, along the southern coast of Crete. Paul thought they should play it safe, stay put in the nearest anchorage, a place which would come to be known as Fair Haven.

The sailing master thought otherwise. He thought they should get the vessel as far across the island as possible, even if it meant facing the danger of sailing along the southern coast. He envisioned lean and hard days ahead, for he knew the high probability that the ship would be caught on that shore for the winter and remain there until spring. He was no near-do-well dredged up from the streets of Alexandria. He knew the sea. He knew the stories told by heart, never written down, but repeated at each port. He was a tried and tested pilot, a professional sailor hired in Myra for this trip, and the captain agreed with him. Julius, too, decided the sailing master knew best. Paul was outvoted.

The writer of Acts does not report the details nor does he make any editorial comment about the final decision; we are, therefore, left to our own deductions. It seems safe to say that a ship of that size would have been manned by a large crew, some of whom may have been promised a percentage of the profits or perhaps threatened with "no voyage completion discharge papers - no pay." At any rate, with the long hard winter looming ahead on the coast of Crete, it's a safe bet that the captain and sailing master wanted to keep the crew happy. They would have wanted to spend the winter in a harbor where there were wine, women, and song.

The next morning when a light wind blew up from the sands of North Africa, the crew unfurled the vast sail for the thirty-seven mile voyage to Phoenix, the wintering spot the captain and the sailing master had in mind. The passengers stood along the deck watching the activity. They could smell the fresh soup simmering and the bread baking back on the stern's clay galley. The event took on a holiday spirit as the entertainers bound for Nero's court decided to do what they did best: sing, play their flutes, and dance. Only the slaves and criminals, those condemned to fight the leopards and lions in the Colosseum, remained below, chained to the benches with the smell of sour grain and the stench of the bilge.

Although there was excitement and noise and revelry around them on deck, some of the passengers must have seen the squall coming; they must have been suspicious when they saw dark clouds forming over the craggy shores and the mountain tops seven thousand feet above the island. The crew must have heard the winds swooping through the deep gorges of the wild terrain. It roars today as if forced through a tunnel. Young trees on the mountainside grow gnarled and leafless in the wind. When the sailing master saw the storm forming, he knew all too well the fury that was coming and he turned the ship to run before the wind. With powerful arms, he held the two steering paddles to control the ship's course in the winds coming from behind.

The crew rushed to shortened the sail. They herded the passengers below, pushed them, terrified and screaming, out of the way and down the ship's hatches. Within seconds the crew was working furiously, wrapping leather cables around the center of the hull to reinforce the wooden planks and ribs. They were frapping the ship. The danger in a storm, as all ancients knew, was not in the winds but in the water that might seep through the weakened planks, waves that might rip through the ribs and lay the vessel open to the seas.

With the frapping done, they lowered the yard, the heavy cross beam at the top of the mast that held the sail. With the large sail lowered and yard lashed to the deck, they raised a small triangular storm sail, a small canvas that allowed the sailing master to turn the boat into the wind, to "lie to," to head into the direction of the wind, drift in the swells but lose little ground, maintain some degree of control, they hoped . . . .

This is a skillful maneuver well-known to any sailor with a mind to keep his boat afloat and undamaged. Steve used this maneuver in a gale near the Azores in the North Atlantic. When the winds reached thirty knots, he lowered his mainsail, raised his storm jib, and turned RISE into the wind. After tying the wheel in place with a shock cork, he went below to ride out the storm in comfort. That's when he played a game of solitaire, and Susan did her aerobic exercises. But Steve had a compass, a radio, and a GPS that charted his course and showed him his precise location. He knew the rate and the direction he was drifting.

The good captain of the Alexandrian grain-boat didn't even have a compass. That handy navigational instrument would not be common place for another thirteen centuries. There was certainly no chart available unless it was guess work drawn on a piece of fig bark. It would be another century before Ptolemy listed the co-ordinates of latitude and longitude of the Earth and another twelve centuries before the Byzantine monks drew charts. With no knowledge of their location, the ship drifted for fourteen days. "Neither the sun nor stars were visible," according to Luke's record. There was no landmark to give them any indication of their position. Obviously they were in no ordinary squall; it was a full-fledged *gregale*, a Greek wind that Pliny the Elder, a Roman admiral, called the "chief pest of seamen."

It was the kind of wind that confined the President of the United States, the chief commander of the mightiest navy in the twentieth century, to his ship in December 1989, the kind of wind that forced George Bush to postpone dinner with Soviet President Mikhail S. Gorbachev during the Maltese summit. The winds held the two presidents captives aboard their respective ships for two days while the world watched their plight on television.

Historians say that ancient mariners may have lost more ships in these ferocious winds than in battle. The Romans had the right idea and scheduled naval battles only in spring or in summer.

Back on the Alexandrian grain boat, the worst was yet to come: The wind pressure on the mast and the pounding of the seas were too much for the hull; and in spite of the undergirding or the frapping, water began seeping through the boards. Because the corn and wheat, wet with sea water, began to swell in the hold, all able bodied passengers were put to work casting the grain overboard. The sea around the ship was stained the color of wheat.

Finally the captain ordered that the foresail be taken down. The ship would have to drift under bare poles, run with the seas; they would have to take what was coming. Drifting under bare poles could run up the miles, perhaps in the wrong direction, but at least they would stay afloat for a while longer. In addition, the captain ordered that the ship be stripped. All extra weight had to go: all bedding handed up and cast over the rails, all ship furniture, extra spars, all rigging, all personal belongings, everything but the clothes on the backs of the passengers. Meanwhile there was real trouble down below. The ship was taking on water by the tons and they had no pumps like modern boats, just a lot of terrified passengers handing up buckets, bailing out the water that poured in. The chronicler of Acts recorded the hopelessness of the situation: " . . . all hope that we should be saved was gradually taken away."

To add to the captain's worries, he heard the crew was planning to lower the long boat in the dead of night and make a getaway. There were rumors of mutiny.

The air below was heavy, thick, and salty. Seasickness was a nightmare. The passengers were sick with their own vomit. Beasts and crew, slaves and freedmen, captives and captors were all thrown together in the horror of unimaginable conditions on a sinking ship.

In the midst of the turmoil, Paul walked below, calming crew and passengers. He would not let go of hope. Perhaps he knew if they were to be saved, the crew needed encouragement. Scholars believe he had been shipwrecked three times before. He, therefore, knew the crew had to remain calm, the captain in full control. "Not one of you shall be lost," he kept telling the passengers as he walked among these crowded below shivering from fright and chill. It is a tribute to his ability as a leader that he calmed the passengers and the crew. They believed him, the man who wore his wet woolen cloak wrapped around him like a mantel and speaking as if had some mysterious power to save them.

Like a miracle, on the fourteenth night there was a lull in the storm, and the crew heard the sound of pounding surf in the distance, an especially ominous sound in the middle sea, for if they had drifted south to North Africa, they would be buried in the quick sands. On the other hand, if they drifted upon rocks, the ship would splinter upon contact and sink to the bottom within seconds. The crew let out sea anchors, ropes with leaden weights that could hold the ship steady until daylight. The captain directed the operation and at dawn they spotted a rocky shore, but it was a land they did not recognize.

This time there was no decision to be made. There was only one course of action: the captain gave the signal and the crew raised the foresail again, just enough canvas to drive the ship onto the rocks. Better to drive the ship upon an unknown shore, the captain decided, than to drift back out to sea, better to sink in a place of his own choosing. From a nautical point of view it was a decision that was impeccable.

As the captain expected, the ship splintered on impact, and as the weakened hull began to break in the middle, the fierce cracking of timber is easy to imagine. Members of the crew were abandoning the ship, leaping into the water, although the captain had commanded them to stay with the vessel. In the chaos, a dreadful yell came from the hold where prisoners were chained. Julius, the Roman in charge, gave the command: "Let the men out. Let the prisoners go," he shouted, brandishing his sword. "Take to the water," he commanded all prisoners, "Go."

There was wild scrambling up from the hold of the ship and down the ropes, some hanging over the sides, some diving naked into the water. Within minutes the sea around the ship was filled with bobbing heads "some on planks, and some on pieces from the ship. And so it came to pass that all escaped safe to the land," recorded the biblical writer who gives Paul full credit for saving the people.

9
The Haven of My Desire

Crete has always been more than just another island in the Mediterranean. To geologists Crete is the southern rim of the great dry basin that flooded five and one half million years ago when the Atlantic roared through the Pillars of Hercules. To ancient mariners the island was buried in mystery and intrigue at the edge of the universe.

Homer wrote: "Out in the wine-dark sea there is a rich and lovely island called Crete." He said the island was "washed by the waves on every side, densely populated with ninety cities . . ."

A Roman said to be the first novelist described Crete as a refuge, a sanctuary. "This is the haven of my quiet desire," Petronius Arbiter wrote after a visit to the island, "Yes, I have lived! Nor can an unkind fate take from me ever gifts of that former hour."

The twentieth century writer, Nikos Kazantzakis, immortalized its people when he created Zorba, the hero who reflects the wild and haunting beauty of Crete.

Mythologically speaking, Zeus was born on its mountain tops. Monsters lurk in its dark and endless caves. The Minotaur, half man and half bull, was confined in its famous labyrinth, a complicated series of tunnels and windings. Daedalus, the architect of the labyrinth escaped being imprisoned there, but Icarus, his son, soared with man-made wings so close to the sun that the wax holding his wings melted, and he plunged into the Cretan Sea.

Europe gets its name from a mythical princess taken to Crete upon the back of a bull that swam with powerful strokes over the sea. "Where do you take me?" she cried.

"I am Zeus," he said, "and I am taking you to Crete to be my bride. Crete is where I was born. Crete shall be our bridal chamber," Zeus told Princess Europa. Because of this union Crete and Europe are forever bound together, according to the myth.

It was to Crete that Theseus sailed to avenge the deaths of the Atheneans, seven noblemen and seven maidens who were given in tribute to King Minos each year and devoured by the Minotaur. This time when the seven men and seven maidens were brought before King Minos, Theseus was among them.

"You, too, will meet your fate," the king told Theseus. The king's daughter, however, was filled with pity and desire for the handsome Theseus. That evening she managed to pass two objects to him: a sword and a ball of thread.

The next morning Theseus was ready for the Minotaur. With the sword he slew the monster and with the ball of thread he escaped by following the thread which he had fastened to the gate. Safely at the harbor, he raised the black sails on his ship and escaped.

Historically speaking, the island was the site of the earliest civilization in the Aegean, the Minoans. It was a highly developed society that existed two thousand years before the Greek classical era, according to archaeologists. It was the grandson of King Minos who led eighty ships across the middle sea to sack the city of Troy. The little seafaring nation was a world power long before the glory days of Athens.

The Romans ignored Crete. They saw the island as wild, its people untamable. The Venetians used it as a strategic location from which to dominate the seas. The Turks overpowered its people for two centuries, controlled its coast, and used its ports as a stepping stone to Spain.

Crete was our destination. We would follow in the wake of the apostle until we, too, spied the twin peaks of Mount Ada and Mount Ditka above the clouds. The similarities in our voyages would stop there, for we had no desire to float with the current down to the southern coast. Present-day charts and sailing guides warn boats about the winds there. Instead, using our engine and modern technology we sailed directly into the capital, a pleasant harbor tucked inside safe harbor walls on the northern shore.

By that time in their voyage to the West, Steve and Susan had much work to do on the boat and plans to make for the next leg of their trip. While they spent their time refueling and adding provisions, I explored Crete. One night I came back to the boat with a new hat cocked jauntily over my forehead and my hand touching something special at my neck. I made no effort to wipe away the smile.

"Mom, you okay?" Susan must have seen a sparkle in my eye.

"Yeah, Mom. What's up?" Steve stopped sanding the boom and looked at me warily, as if he suspected his mother of selling the family jewels. "Where have you been?"

How could I tell them? How could I explain that a man so spontaneous, so unable to deceive, so honest with his feelings – a man I didn't know and would never see again – a Cretan had made me happy those few days. He had made me laugh. A Greek had made me feel carefree, young enough to dance, to dream again.

Our rendezvous began innocently enough. I was sitting in the back of the church of Agai Akaterini admiring the frescoes painted by a famous Greek artist. Highly polished bronze and brass glittered in the sunlight all around.

He sat beside me, a Cretan hardly as handsome as Zorba; in fact, he was nothing at all like the main character in the movie I had seen years before. This Zorba was stout and heavy and broad-boned; he was of a different stock, with a short and stubborn neck. His complexion was ruddy and flushed, but his eyes were so dark and intent they could pierce any woman's soul.

"English?" he asked, watching me thoughtfully.

"American," I told him.

He had a sister in America, he whispered, looking at me steadily. "Will you drink Raki with me?" he asked.

I had heard about that potent drink. I might be brave enough to wander alone on the streets of that mysterious island and even talk to strangers, but I was not about to drink Raki with a native. I suspected there was more than innocent intentions in the invitation.

"Retsini?" he asked, undressing me with his eyes as only a Greek can do.

I declined and when his smile faded in the silence, I was embarrassed. Perhaps I was being impolite, too aloof. I was not in the habit of making casual conversation with men. Perhaps I should be more friendly, I decided.

"Bira," I suggested. I'd have a beer with him. What could be the harm in having a beer with a Cretan on a hot summer day in Greece?

"A beer?" I asked again in case he had not understood my Greek.

A guttural sound escaped from his lips. His eyes widened, sudden and intense, as if he were in pain. "No-o-o-o," he whispered. "No, no bed," he said; his face darkening in a painfully embarrassed flush.

"No beer?" I didn't understand. I was innocent, but there was a definite lack of communication here.

"No beer?" I asked, adding to the awkwardness of the moment.

"No bed." He stood to leave.

"No bed?" I was stunned. "You misunderstand," I shouted, ignoring the tourists wandering up and down the aisle. *"Bira. Bira,* not bed." The tourists glared.

He asked me to lunch and we drank Amstel. We ate pistachio under the plane trees in the city square. He showed me how to pick the fruit from the green fern-like plant to find the nuts. We were cautious and proper.

"Yesterday I saw you," he admitted. "Today I follow you into the church."

"Why?" I was astonished.

"Do I have to have a reason? In Crete a man can admire a woman without a reason. Because he wants to. That is why. I have a question. Why you are alone?"

I told him about my marriage of forty years, about the loss of a husband to cancer. My voice gave way to a lifetime of memories and a grief I thought I had overcome. He said helplessly, "I am sorry."

"Tell me about yourself," I said, determined to recover. "Tell me about life on Crete."

He, too, had experienced loss. His wife and infant son had died years before in an automobile accident. He had gone to the mainland to work and forget, but he had come back to Crete.

"Life here is good. The Greek way on Crete is good," he

said. "I come back to my take care of my mother. She is old. I come back to roots, to put my life in boxes."

"Boxes?"

"Yes, boxes. It is the Cretan way. In biggest box, largest box I keep my roots, my family." He made a box with his hands to show its large dimensions. "You know?" I nodded to let him know I understood that he put family first in his life.

"In the next big box," he stopped to form a smaller box with his hands. "I keep friends," he said and I nodded again.

"Then, in smaller box I put my books."

"You like to read?"

"Yes. I keep my books with me everywhere I go. And then . . . in smallest box . . . ," he said, holding up his thumb and index finger to indicate a box as small as a match box. "In smallest box. Tiny box. I place work." He laughed and shrugged his shoulders. "That is life on Crete. That is the Greek way."

At that moment I admired the Cretan attitude and remembered a line from the German poet who also admired the Greek way. "Of all peoples, the Greeks have dreamt the dream of life best," Goethe wrote.

That afternoon he took me to Knossos. We walked through the grand entrance of the palace of the Minoans with its bright red columns and sky blue stucco, commanding the attention it did millennia ago when King Minos ruled the seas. Spiral staircases lead to the four levels of the palace. Light wells captured the sun rays at just the right angle to spotlight the finely painted frescoes with natural lighting. One vast room was still filled with earthenware jars, some more than six feet high, once filled with grain, oil, dried fish or olives.

"The original frescoes are in the museum," he told me. He was a knowledgeable tour guide, as all Greeks are. "These are identical to the pieces found in the excavation." He seemed excited to once again tell the story of Knossos.

In the late nineteenth century a Cretan archaeologist struck the massive palace that had been buried for thousands of years, he said. The fragments tell the story of broad-shouldered, slim-waisted priests and proud aristocratic cup-bearers of the ancient civilization. He showed me fragments of Minoan ladies sitting in jeweled garments toying with glittering necklaces, their long black hair as elaborately coiffured as hair styles of the French court. He showed me pictures of thin, athletic youth somersaulting over the back of the sacred bulls, practicing acrobatics.

In the fourteenth century BC the palace buzzed with artisans, potters and joiners. On the streets could be heard the noise of forges and oil presses. Priests and priestesses chanted to the Great Mother Goddess creating some unknown supernatural connection with the libation jug, the double axe or the sacred bough, a connection even my new friend had not figured out. We know only that the Minoans were a peace loving, seafaring people who preferred theater and music, festivals and games to sacking cities and waging war.

Then one spring day amid the typical flurry of activity around the palace, time ran out for the oldest civilization in the Aegean. Some archaeologists say the calamity was caused by an earthquake. Others say a volcanic eruption on another island spewed hot ash into the air to ignite a fire that demolished Knossos and crippled the nation forever.

Perhaps the disaster was a natural catastrophe. No one knows, but as we stood in the great throne room, it was easy for us to imagine the sound of retaliation and violence when the great jars filled with ritual oils overturned and shattered, when the massive gypsum benches surrounding the chamber splintered into shards. Only the throne itself escaped untouched – only the giant sculptured stone, the seat of Minos the king, remained intact after the cataclysmic event.

"The real throne is in the museum in Athens, as it was found here in the excavation," he whispered.

As the setting sun turned the palace courtyard the color of gold, my friend quoted Kazantzakis: "In old ruined cities, the air is filled with cries and the noise of spirits." We tiptoed down the steps of the palace. "If a branch cracks, if a lizard darts, if a cloud throws a shadow as it passes overhead, panic seizes you." I stood listening to the wind in the olive trees. "Every inch of ground you tread is a grave," he whispered, "and you hear the dead groaning." Around us there were other tourists listening with us. No one spoke until we reached the parking lot.

I said nothing to Steve and Susan but met the Greek early the next day. We drove to the mountains, the birthplace of Zeus. "Lord of the sky," he shouted, the wind blowing through the open windows, "God of the thunderbolt," he explained.

I nodded. "Most great God of the storm clouds."

"Thou that dwellest in the heavens."

"I teach Homer," I told him.

"Every Greek knows lines from *The Iliad*," he said.

In the villages dark-eyed girls sat in their doorways crocheting and embroidering delicate linens "for the bazaars" he said. Old men sat under the plane trees drinking coffee and playing cards, mountain men wearing tight fitting trousers tucked inside tall boots.

"Mountaineer boots. The trade mark of the klefts, the rebels who took to the mountains when foreigners came by sea," he explained. "They banded together and kept in touch with each other and the mainland. The klefts were the first to demand "enos," freedom from the Turks," he said, his hands gripping the wheel, his face turning serious, his eyes narrowing.

"Our island is Greek. We declare our freedom from the Turks. We revolt and we never forget the cruelty, the atrocities," he said. "I want to show you Arkadi."

Around the next mountain, he stopped the car at a monastery where hundreds of women and children died rather than surrender to the Turks. "For two days they hold out against three thousand. But the Turks stormed the refectory. When that happened, the priests ordered the torch be put to the powder magazine. Three hundred were martyred, but the Turks were turned back and the monastery was saved. It is where we celebrate our independence."

We stood in the courtyard of the monastery surrounded by a quadrangle. The rooms were empty when we were there. Only three aging monks lived there. Once there would have been a hundred murmuring the ancient Greek Orthodox rituals. I followed my friend to a small chapel where he knelt before the bones of Abbott Gabriel, the monk who sacrificed three hundred innocent lives for the freedom of all Cretans.

Later we drank tea and sat on stone benches near the chapel, the noon-day sun turning everything around us honey-colored.

"A man needs freedom," he said, sniffing his tea, holding his cup with his thumb and his index finger, the oriental way, as I had seen Turkish men do. He seemed deep in thought. "Greeks always fight to be free," he said. "We fought to be free of the Nazis."

"What was it like during the war? Here on Crete, I mean?"

"I don't remember."

"But you must remember something."

"Some things I don't want to talk about. Like the war."

We were quiet for a long time. "How old were you?"

"Nine," he said, his voice tight. "I was nine years old when the Allies came. The sky was filled with parachutes. The wounded were lying in the streets of my village. They were bleeding. My brother took my father's caique and filled it with the British paratroopers. He smuggled them out to the Allied destroyers. I was too young to help. He wouldn't let me go with him."

He walked away, stood looking at the chapel then turned back to me, "But I watched from the shore," he told me. "There were many trips. Five. Maybe six. Then just before dawn, the Germans spotted the caique. It was my father's fishing boat. It was small. My brother never returned."

I could think of nothing to say. We drove to the south of the island, the wild, southern coast that faced Libya. He said pirates had invaded that coast of Crete at will. They had killed the farmers and slaughtered the sheep. They stole the grain and raped the women, bound them with their red belts and threw them in the hold of ships then sailed away to sell them in Alexandria or Sidon or Algiers. Cretan women are still shy and distrustful of foreigners, he said and it is true: they rarely speak to tourists.

"Saint Paul," I whispered as we parked beside the highway looking over the southern coast of the island. The water looked calm and serene.

"Yes, I show you the coast of saints and sinners. It is the coast of the apostle."

He pointed to the desolate coast below. "There to the left is where Saint Paul's ship first lay at anchor. It is called Fair

Haven. And to the right as far as you can see. Can you see the tiny settlement at the water's edge?"

"Yes. Across the gulf."

"That is Phoenix. That is where the ship was heading when the storm roared down from these cliffs and swept the ship out to sea."

I could see no modern cruise ship anchored there, no tiny sailboat following in the wake of the Alexandrian grain boat. There was nothing but the sea, only a vast expanse of water stretching across the horizon to Africa.

I walked ahead along the craggy precipice listening to the sounds, and when I looked back, he had taken off his shoes and rolled up his trousers. Like the Zorba I had seen in the movie, he stood with his arms held high over his head, his palms open, crying out, "Krite. Krite. Krite." He danced and I followed his steps until we were both out of breath and laughing.

"You love Crete, don't you?" We lay back on the grass listening to the sounds below.

"I love everything about it. Like the poet says, 'It is the haven of desire.' It is my home. I love the scent of the sea surrounding my home. Can you smell it? It is sweet like a melon. I love the sound. Can you feel the passion? Can you hear it? The sea."

"It sighs." I could hear no surf but a soft hum from the sea below, a moan.

"Yes, it sighs like a woman. It moans with the pleasure a man can give a woman."

For reasons I did not understand, I wanted to stand and cry out across the sea. I wanted to create the sound that I held in my heart. It would have been a sound filled with love for the sea and the air around me, so filled with gratitude for my children, those with me and those at home, that Poseidon would have answered from his throne below. I wanted to tell the world how I felt, but I held it back, knowing that in the land of the Greeks, one is easily transported from reality to dream. It is, after all, a land filled with gods and goddesses of passion, all things sensual. I held my breath and said nothing. In silence we watched the sea change from aubergine to indigo blue.

My friend had another stop to make, one more thing he wanted to show me. "You know Saint Titus' well? Titus is our patron saint, you know." He stopped at an olive orchard half-way down the mountain and we walked to a well where he pulled the ropes that raised and lowered the buckets into the ground. He insisted that I place drachmes in the bucket. "For good luck," he said, lighting a candle and saying a prayer to the saint they believe brought Christianity to Crete. I followed his example, knowing that in that part of the world it's important to have the protection of the gods.

"You need protection from the evil eye," he said, his dark eyes so intent that I looked away.

"What do you mean?" I asked, afraid of his answer.

"I give you good luck charm." He spoke softly. "You will wear it?"

Of course I would. I had noticed the charms worn by Cretan women: a small blue eye worn on a gold chain. It was worn as more than jewelry, I could tell. I had supposed it conjured up magic to keep the darker forces away. He took a charm from his pocket and gently, reverently clasped it around my neck. "You should not be alone," he said. "There is much inside you, much for a man to admire."

I turned to walk back to the car, and he called out in the dark, "You must wear it, even in America," he said, taking a step forward then stopping. "You need protection from the evil spirits." When I turned back, his eyes were glistening. I knew he was smiling.

I smiled, too, and it may have been my imagination; of course, it was my imagination, but when I returned to the boat that night, I thought I moved with a new-found serenity, a tranquility that comes with security and self-confidence. Perhaps it was the sure protection of the gods. Looking back, I know it was a turning point for me. My fear of the future was gone, not reasoned away but warded off by magic and that was okay by me, for when I put my hand to my neck to touch the charm, I felt the old confidence. I felt young again.

I do to this day. I touch the charm to feel the magic. I often remember that afternoon, and when I do, I hear the sound of the Cretan sea sighing. I smell it sweet like a melon and remember the colors as they turned ever-so-slowly from aubergine to indigo blue.

10
Off the Record

The biblical record is brief and to the point: the Alexandrian grain boat sank off an island in the middle sea and the passengers, along with the crew, spent the winter waiting for another ship, one large enough to take all three hundred or so to Rome. All else is conjecture, but we know that the island was Malta, a place in the Mediterranean with a history of shipwrecks and storms. It was there that Odysseus landed after his ship wrecked fourteen centuries before Paul. A storm hit his black ship when the winds hurled down off the mountains of Sicily and "snapped both the forestays."

Odysseus's helmsman wasn't as lucky as the helmsman on the grain boat, for the mast on Odysseus's ship collapsed and smashed his skull. The ship undoubtedly turned broadside to the waves and according to Homer, "men were flung overboard and tossed around the black hull like sea-gulls on the waves." Like the grain boat, Odysseus's boat disintegrated, the planks opened up to the sea, and the ribs gave way, but Odysseus managed to grab onto the planks and float to safety on a makeshift raft. "Nine days of drifting followed . . . on the night of the tenth day thanks to the gods I was washed ashore on the island . . . the home of the fair Calypso . . . ." Most scholars and sailors agree that Malta was the home of the fair Calypso.

Except for the few lines written in the biblical Christian account, what we know about Paul's life after the shipwreck is based on tradition, oral history handed down from islanders around the middle sea and information that biblical scholars extrapolate from the letters Paul is believed to have written while in Rome.

After the storm the passengers quickly gathered around the man who stayed with them. It's easy to imagine them bowing, kissing his hand, prostrating themselves on the ground in Eastern fashion, thanking him for saving them from a sure and terrible death. It's just as easy to imagine Paul accepting their praise, their adoration, viewing the disaster as a miracle, a challenge, an opportunity to form a congregation on Malta.

The islanders listened. They were kind but suspicious of the foreigner. Perhaps that was the reason Paul turned to magic. The story goes that when a snake inadvertently wrapped itself around his arm, he worked a miracle. It's true that snakes were plentiful on islands. The vipers were no doubt hiding in the underbrush as the shivering passengers gathered branches, palm fronds, anything to protect themselves against the rain and the wind. It was said that only the light of small fires could keep snakes away from the beach.

"Beware," the natives whispered to each other, watching and waiting when they saw the snake wrap itself around Paul's arm.

"He's a magician," some said. "A sorcerer," the islanders warned.

"It's a sign of evil," they whispered as Paul took the snake from his arm, held it by the head and flung it into a fire. He stood before them unharmed.

"It is a sign," the shout went up. "He is not an evil spirit. He is good. Evil is consumed in the fire."

To this day in that part of the Mediterranean the islands are free of snakes. They say because Paul was there. They say the famous missionary cleansed the island of vipers.

It is also said that one warm day in spring, sails appeared like a vision on the horizon, a ship on its way to Puteoli and the port at Rome. The passengers ran to the shore waving their arms. The crew climbed on top of the highest rock to signal to the passing ship and Julius the Centurion was sent out to bargain with the ship captain. Once again he struck a deal and hustled his prisoners out to the ship then up the rope ladder that hung from its sides.

Paul was, at last, on his way to Rome, a haven for sinners, the capital of the pagan world. He arrived tired and stooped, the final sail from Malta having taken longer than usual. He was a prisoner, after all, and was expected to march from the port of Rome at the head of the column of prisoners chained to Julius the Centurion. Outside the city at the Via Appia he nodded to the small delegation sent out to meet him, the quiet followers already practicing the new religion: a few tradesmen from Asia Minor, sandal makers from Corinth, silver smiths from Cyprus, the small band of faithful who had heard he was coming. Word had spread throughout the Jewish quarters that Paul was coming, but no one knew why. There had been no letter of warning, no message from those who were bringing the charges back in Jerusalem.

The procession of prisoners with the shipwrecked passengers tagging behind probably moved through the city gates at Porta Appia. They made their way through the marketplace of the poor, the *subura*, where a mixture of races and religions, slaves and freedmen lived, for Caesar had brought them to Rome from every frontier. A babel of tongues rose like smoke from the braziers, sounds mixing with the sour smell of unwashed linen and old wool. Nearby the odor of garbage escaped from the openings to the Cloaca Maxima, the giant sewer system that emptied outside the city gates into the Tiber.

If he looked up from his chains, Paul would have been stunned by the mixture of cultures, ideologies, and goods: blond Germans pulling two-wheeled carts loaded with large jars of grain, red-headed Britons dragging blocks of marble, and powerfully built Slavs lifting limestone boulders. Along the side streets there were Chaldaean snake charmers and Syrian wine dealers. The procession found itself weaving through booths pushed into the middle of the streets, wooden trays filled with dried meat, salted fish and sausages.

There is no doubt but that Julius would have marched his prisoners straight to the headquarters of the Imperial Guard, turned them over, and headed for the baths. That is precisely what any soldier would have done, certainly one who had served a tour of duty in the rocky, dusty, barren country called Judaea. For his service in the outer provinces, there were perks. Luxurious baths were reserved for the elite guard. There were, of course, the public baths where ordinary Romans scalded and steamed their bodies. Then, there were the baths used by the senators and emperors, gilded and marbled baths where half a day could be spent luxuriating in water scented with Arabian perfume, rubbed with aromatic Asian oils, anointed with Judaean balsams, and wrapped in Persian silk. The baths of the elite guard were enough for Julius.

Scholars agree that Paul was probably placed under guard in a small room with a mat for sleeping and a table for writing. He was given private quarters, they say, but the reasons are still unclear. It was perhaps his privilege as a

Roman citizen. Some stories say a wealthy Jewish merchant intervened in his behalf. Certainly bribery was not uncommon in the corrupt Roman courts of the day. One tradition says that someone close to Caesar, someone like the well-known Seneca, intervened with the proposition that Paul was harmless because his message was beamed to the lowest of people, the Jews. The message was about one of their own who died the lowest of deaths and crucified like a slave. Seneca could have argued that Paul's messages would actually make the slaves, who swarmed over the city, more obedient, make them more subservient.

At any rate, by the time the passengers on the ill-fated ship, arrived in Rome, Nero's latest wedding had come and gone, leaving Caesar more morose and distracted than ever. He was writing poetry. Patricians were critiquing and declaiming, sounding like professors as they quoted from *The Odyssey* and *The Iliad.* Night after night senators sat bored into oblivion listening to Nero's mediocre, mundane verse.

Meanwhile affairs of state were pretty much at a stand still and when Paul's case was heard in the court system five years later, an unknown tribune probably heard the case. There is no evidence that the plaintiffs, the Jews from Judaea, appeared; instead, Paul defended himself, as was the Greek custom, and was set free, according to the beliefs of many. If so, he was at liberty to travel again. Islanders say he sailed back to the island of Malta, and on Crete they say he came back to visit the spot where he was swept away. Many believe he crossed over to Asia Minor to visit the congregations there.

If tradition is right, Paul was on one of those trips when Rome burned. The Roman historian Tacitus dates the burning to the summer of 64 AD; that's when fire broke out in the oil and flour depots around the thickly populated area of the Circus Maximus. For nine days the fire raged and Tacitus says that rumors spread quickly that the fire had been set deliberately – by none other than Nero himself. It is also Tacitus who connects the burning to the persecution of the new class of people who practiced a new superstition, a magic, he said; they were a menace to the commonwealth, he recorded.

With rumors flying, Caesar no doubt gathered his aides together for a meeting and threatened them with death unless they devised a plan and a good one at that. Today we would call the plan "damage control." Their task: to deflect attention away from Nero, to recast the facts. To find a "shield issue," an inflammatory, emotion-packed issue to shield Caesar from the rumors. To find a scapegoat.

What better scapegoat could there be than the Jews, those who refused to worship the Roman gods, those who refused to recognize Caesar as a god? They were the most alien from the distant provinces. The weakest. The most despised. What a brilliant idea, the aides said to each other, pleased with their own ingenuity. The gods are angry, they told Caesar. The gods are aghast at the destruction of the temples and appalled at the arrogance of the Jews. The Jews caused the fire. The Jews are to blame. The Jews and their magic, their invisible God, the aides told Caesar, shaking their heads and using words like calamity, pestilence, placate, atonement – words like guilty, punish, torture, revenge, blood, slaughter. Nero smiled his malevolent smile and ordered that the plan be put in place.

Tacitus describes the torture and persecution, the mockery of the Jews, the years of ethnic cleansing. Whether they were converts to the new religion or not, Jews were rounded up, stripped naked, and driven into the arena to face wild oxen and blood hounds, although historians clearly believe they were innocent of the burning. The prevailing view is that Nero set the city on fire.

Nevertheless, a killing frenzy spread out to the provinces, and according to legend, Paul was arrested again while he was visiting a congregation in Troas and charged with spreading the forbidden doctrine. When he was returned to Rome, he refused to offer incense before the image of Nero. This time he stood before the tribunal without his mantle. He stretched his stooped and broken body, and admitted calmly, "I am a Christian."

He made no appeal as a Roman citizen. Instead, he acted as if he believed in only one life and that one life passed from this world to the next. They say he showed no fear, although he was swiftly condemned and placed in an underground dungeon along with hundreds of other Jews taken in the catacombs. Much is speculation; however, this much is definite: Paul was beheaded with the dignity given to a Roman citizen. Historians agree to that, but legend can point to the very spot he was beheaded just outside the city gates on the Via Ostiensis.

11
The Winds of Change

Twenty centuries after Paul was swept away from Crete's southern shore in the Greek *gregale*, Steve and Susan sailed away from its northern shore in twenty-knot winds, the kind that could take RISE all the way to Cythera and into the Adriatic. They planned to continue the ancient course by following the old sailing route to Rome, but first they must head for that point of land all the ancients prayed they could reach – Cythera. Many a mariner had missed it.

The captain of the Alexandrian grain boat had missed it. Fifteen centuries before that, Odysseus had missed it, and he was an experienced sea captain. After making a name for himself as a famous sacker of cities, he returned from Troy but missed the strategic island and spent seven more years wandering around the middle sea at the mercy of the gods.

He had left Asia Minor victorious and still in command of his squadron of ships, probably twelve, all open boats, shallow-drafted and keel-less. It is believed that each boat had a crew of twenty, with ten rowers on each side. Considering his need for fresh crew members and his crew's propensity for piracy, it is possible that Odysseus left Troy with a force of as many as five hundred men.

He left the continent north of Knidos where the grain boat was stalled before catching the strong current flowing south. Odysseus wanted no part of Crete, which was to the ancients the edge of the universe. No doubt he chose to stick close to the mainland of Greece, then use a channel between Euboea and Athens. After that, he planned to island hop – just as the grain boat captain planned to do – until he could make the dash for Cythera where he would turn his fleet north into the Adriatic and sail home to Ithaca.

But the wind was coming from the wrong direction, driving him from Troy and sending him north to the city of Ismarus. The war, which had lasted for ten years, was no doubt still in his blood. Besides, he had five hundred men to appease; so, according to Homer, his troops sacked the next city they saw, which happened to be Ismarus, divided the loot, and took the bounty. He came out of the raid with gold talents, a silver bowl and seven jars of the best Ismarian wine.

Odysseus would learn, however, that on the sea he was not always so lucky. Within hours the wind shifted, a *meltemi* came out of the north, and sent his fleet scurrying for safety. The crews rowed as hard as they could for the island of Euboea where they could haul their boats ashore, but they couldn't make it. Experienced sailors who have sailed that way and been caught in those same winds say that his ships were swept below the island. One such sailor is Ernle Bradford who in the early nineteen sixties sailed the Med for seven years, visiting all the places Homer described, testing the winds and currents, navigating as the ancients did. He believes that Odysseus was swept to the tip of Euboea, where he island hopped, and like the grain boat captain and present-day sailors like Steve and Susan, he planned to make a dash for Cythera.

Like the grain boat captain, he never made it. The current running down the Adriatic took his ships farther and farther from land and though he undoubtedly put all his men to the oars, they could not round the point at Cythera and get into sheltered water. As fate would have it, the winds picked up and turned into the dreaded *gregale*, the same winds that swept Paul's ship away from Crete. His fleet drifted south like the Alexandrian grain boat and when the storm ceased nine days later, Odysseus and his men found themselves on the shores of North Africa; Bradford says near Lybia; Homer called those shores the Land of the Lotus-Eaters.

Thus begins the tale of Odysseus, the explorer, and the stories we all know: the cruel Cyclopes (Sicily); Circe's island (a point of land on the coast of Italy mistaken for an island); the Sirens (The Galli Islands off the coast of Italy); Scylla and Charybdis (the Straits of Messina) and Calypso's island (Malta). Recorded for posterity is the story of the first Greek to explore the Western Mediterranean, the first Greek to glimpse the Pillars of Hercules and the Stream of Ocean. Homer says ". . . she (Circe) brought us to the deep River of Ocean and the frontier of the world." It was a sight which must have struck terror in the heart of even brave Odysseus, as well as the hearts of many an ancient mariner. Odysseus had lost all but one ship by the time he sailed to the end of civilization, the end of the world to the Greeks.

Unknown to the Greeks, the Phoenecians were already out in the Atlantic. They had sailed out of Syria, across the middle sea, and out into the Atlantic to bring back gold and silver and exotic animals but had duped the Greeks to keep them out of the trade routes to the West. The Phoenecians told the Greeks whopping tales of demons and monsters in the River Ocean, stories we hand down in cartoons and children's books to this day. They described the slime and the seaweed and told about a sun so hot it boiled the pitch out of ships and they sank.

The Greeks believed the stories and never traveled out into the Atlantic, except for Odysseus who wandered so far out that he encountered the shades of the dead in the twilight world of Hades. Only then did he return to Ithaca to rout the greedy suitors and save his long-suffering wife, Penelope.

When Steve and Susan left Crete, they were on their way to Ithaca, the island kingdom of Odysseus. There had been long discussions before leaving, intense debates with charts and travel books spread out in the main cabin. Rome would come later, they finally decided, but first they would follow Odysseus' course to the island where Penelope had waited for his return, where she had knitted by day and unraveled by night for seventeen years to put off the suitors who begged for her hand.

My voyage was over. I would fly home to teach my college freshmen who were waiting for me with bated breath, I was sure. Watching RISE leave in the early morning darkness, I tried to surpress memories of all the sea stories. Although Odysseus and the grain boat captain had missed Cythera, I was was sure Steve and Susan would make it - with the protection of Paul's invisible God.

They planned to hug the coast of Crete, then at the westernmost tip of the island cross over to Cythera by harnessing the power of their modern-day engine when the wind was in doubt. They would hug the coast of the Peloponnese, stopping to view the citadel of King Agamemnon and walk among the ghosts in Sparta. They wanted to see what was left of Corinth, the city of sinners that Paul used as a base when he went to Greece. At Ithaca they would anchor in a small natural harbor, the kind of spot where

Odysseus might have hidden when he arrived back home unannounced.

After Greece they would sail up the Adriatic to Yugoslavia, enjoy the beaches and visit its picturesque towns along the coast, but their travels in that part of the Mediterranean were short lived. Their plans were thwarted when artillery shells rained down on the old Medieval city of Debrovnic, and they were forced to sail away in darkness. War had started. It was a matter of life or death as they crossed to Italy with no lights, no radio, no electronics, nothing to give their position away. They sailed, listening for the sound of a diesel engine on a ship of the night, a ship bringing contraband to the warring factions in Croatia and Bosnia.

Along those shores of the Mediterranean the spell had been broken; Yugoslavia was disintegrating. The animosities of a thousand years or more were erupting again. It's a history as old as the middle sea and as dangerous as the winds that blow across those waters.

Acknowledgements

In writing the "Paul" sections of this book, I relied heavily on the scholarly research I found in the library at Erskine Theological Seminary. I am indebted to the librarians there and those at Lander University who also gave willingly of their time when I dashed in with questions. I am grateful to Dr. Gilbert Guinn and Dr. Branimir Reiger, colleagues at Lander, who offered valuable advice early on, and all my other friends at Lander who, along with feedback and advice, gave me encouragement.

I wish to thank the Reverend Clyde Ireland, adjunct professor of religion at the University of South Carolina at Aiken and a life-long friend, for long conversations that helped stimulate the writing of this book.

To Steve and Susan, who invited me along on this leg of their voyage in the Mediterranean, especially Susan who suggested that we follow in the path of Saint Paul and thus planted the seed for this book, I wish to record my thanks, and to all my friends who have listened to excerpts and chapters and urged me to keep writing, I am indebted.

Above all, to R. Bodman of Watermark Publications for his long-suffering and constant confidence, I will forever be grateful.

Back home Steve and Susan have packed away their sailing clothes, resumed careers, and stored their journals. Do they still sense the magic in those seas? I think I can see restlessness in their eyes when they gaze out over the Atlantic from their Sullivan's Island home. Their eyes take on that far-away dreamy quality, especially when they hold their two small daughters, one on each lap, and tell our favorite story: "Once upon a time there was a boat that sailed across the sea to follow in the wake of the ancients . . . ."

Bibliography

I do not propose to give a complete list of the sources I have consulted for this book, but many of the following were on board RISE as we sailed and gave us hours of fascination; the others I have used extensively and enjoyed every one. I think the reader will find all of these captivating reading:

Acton, A. A., **O'er Land and Sea with the Apostle Paul.** Fleming H. Revell Company. London, 1933.

Asch, Sholem. **The Apostle.** G.P. Putnam's Sons. New York, 1943.

Bradford, Ernle. **Paul the Traveller,** Penguin Books. London, 1974.

Bradford, Ernle. **Ulysses Found,** Harcourt Brace & World, Inc., New York,1963.

Braudel Fernand. **The Mediterranean.** Vol.II. Harper and Row. New York,1949. English translation 1973.

Cottrell, Leonard, **The Bull of Minos.** Holt, Rinhart and Winston. New York, 1953.

Hamilton, Edith. **Mythology.** Little, Brown& Company. Boston, Mass. 1940

Herzberg, Max. **Myths and Their Meaning.** Allyn and Bacon. Boston, 1984.

Myres, John L., **Geographical History in Greek Lands.** Greenwood Press. Westport, Conn., 1974.

Pendlebury, J.D.S., **The Archaeology of Crete.** W.W. Norton & Company, Inc. New York, 1965.

Ramsay, W.M., **Saint Paul The Traveller and the Roman Citizen.** Hodder and Stoughton. London, 1905.

Ramsay, W. M. **The Cities of Saint Paul.** Hodder and Stoughton. New York, 1907.

Sewell, Brian, "In the Wake of Cleopatra," **Conde Nast Traveler,** June 1989.

Smith, James. **The Voyage and Shipwreck of Saint Paul.** Baker Book House. Grand Rapids, Michigan, 1978.

Weiss, Johannes. **Earliest Christianity.** Vol.I. Harper and Brothers. New York. 1937.